THE JERSEY SHORE
Including Atlantic City

LAURA KINIRY

Contents

THE JERSEY SHORE

Including Atlantic City

© LAURA KINIRY

THE JERSEY SHORE

For nearly two centuries, New Jersey's 127-mile Atlantic coastline has been a favorite vacation destination for Northeast travelers, and more recently, Canadians and Europeans. There's no denying that the Shore has got it going on. Every summer, New Yorkers and Pennsylvanians clog New Jersey's roadways, along with our own "bennies" and "shoobies," heading towards surf, sun, and fun that only exists along boardwalks and in the shore's casinos, restaurants, bars, and bays. Ladies slick back their locks trying to prevent the inevitable frizz, while guys ditch the suits for flip-flops and shorts. A week's worth of clothes fit into a weekend tote bag—coverage is minimal in the sticky shore heat. Blankets appear along beaches, parked with giant umbrellas and low-slung chairs, as kids break out the buckets and shovels, moms lather on the lotion, and paddleball players pair up along the rising tide. Banner planes advertising dollar drafts and surf-and-turf specials fly slowly overhead.

The Jersey Shore consists mostly of low-lying barrier islands surrounded by back bays and wetlands, although a few towns are located on the mainland. Beaches are sandy, and many have scrub-covered western dunes acting as barriers to high tides and storms. Erosion is a problem all along the shore. Cities and towns are constantly replenishing their beaches with money partially raised through beach tag sales, only to see their efforts washed away with the next big storm. Collecting shells is a popular beach activity. Most beaches are loaded with clam, conch, and oyster shells, and depending on month, the armor of horseshoe crabs and jellyfish.

© LAURA KINIRY

HIGHLIGHTS

◖ Sandy Hook and the Highlands: Where else in New Jersey can you swim in the ocean (naked, if you like) and bask in the backdrop of Manhattan (page 15)?

◖ Spring Lake: Calling to mind the grandeur of the Jersey Shore past, this elegant and classy beachfront town is the perfect spot to take a step back in time (page 32).

◖ Barnegat Lighthouse State Park: Tucked up in Long Beach Island's northern tip, this tiny state park is home to one of New Jersey's most endearing lighthouses, Old Barney, a 217-step watchtower offering unbeatable views (page 43).

◖ Atlantic City's Casinos: Move over, Vegas, the AC is back with a new slew of shopping, restaurants, spas, and hotels. And with its long-established rep as a sparkling senior center, there's nowhere to go but up (page 57).

◖ Lucy the Elephant: New Jersey's iconic pachyderm has weathered well over 100 years along Margate's coast, having done stints as a tavern and private residence before opening up as a museum. With a new coat of paint and freshly touched-up toenails, she has no plans to retire her trunk (page 69).

◖ Ocean City: The best little Shore town on this side of the country. My nephew thinks his granddad owns the boardwalk because of all the time my father spends there. Oh, how I wish he did (page 72).

◖ Wildwoods Boardwalk: As experiences go, this two-mile waterfront stretch – packed with amusements, stuffed prizes, fried-food stands, tacky T-shirt shops, and one of the surliest tram cars around – is unbeatable. Pair it with the neon lights and plastic palms of the surrounding doo-wop motels, and you've got yourself one kitschy weekend (page 84).

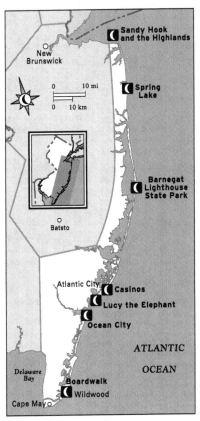

LOOK FOR ◖ TO FIND RECOMMENDED SIGHTS, ACTIVITIES, DINING, AND LODGING.

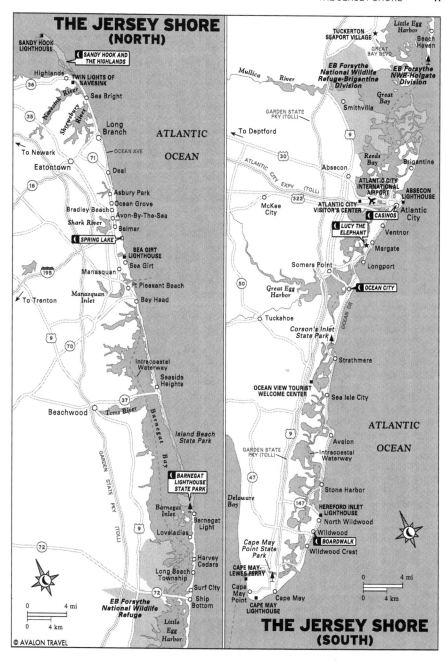

THE JERSEY SHORE
(NORTH)

SANDY HOOK
LIGHTHOUSE

SANDY HOOK AND
THE HIGHLANDS

Highlands
TWIN LIGHTS OF
NAVESINK
36

Sea Bright

35

Long
Branch

ATLANTIC

To Newark
OCEAN AVE

OCEAN

Eatontown
71
Deal

18

Asbury Park
Ocean Grove
Bradley Beach
Avon-By-The-Sea
Shark River
Belmar

SPRING LAKE

SEA GIRT
LIGHTHOUSE
Sea Girt

195

Manasquan

Manasquan
Inlet

Pt Pleasant Beach

To Trenton
Bay Head

9

70

Intracoastal
Waterway

Seaside
Heights

37

Beachwood
Toms River

Barnegat Bay

GARDEN STATE PKY (TOLL)

Island Beach
State Park

BARNEGAT
LIGHTHOUSE
STATE PARK

Barnegat
Inlet

Barnegat
Light

72

Loveladies

Harvey
Cedars

9

Long Beach
Township
Surf City

72

Ship
Bottom

EB Forsythe
National Wildlife
Refuge

Little
Egg
Harbor

0   4 mi

0   4 km

© AVALON TRAVEL

TUCKERTON
SEAPORT VILLAGE
Little Egg
Harbor
Beach
Haven

GREAT
BAY BLVD

Mullica   River

EB Forsythe
National Wildlife
Refuge-Brigantine
Division

EB Forsythe
NWR-Holgate
Division

GARDEN STATE
PKY (TOLL)

Great
Bay

Smithville

To Deptford

9

30

Reeds
Bay

Brigantine

Absecon

ATLANTIC CITY EXPY (TOLL)

ATLANTIC CITY
INTERNATIONAL
AIRPORT

ABSECON
LIGHTHOUSE

322

ATLANTIC CITY
VISITOR'S CENTER

McKee
City

CASINOS

Atlantic
City

LUCY THE
ELEPHANT

Ventnor

Margate

Somers Point

Longport

50

Great Egg
Harbor

OCEAN CITY

Tuckahoe

Corson's Inlet
State Park

OCEAN DR

Strathmere

OCEAN VIEW TOURIST
WELCOME CENTER

Sea Isle City

ATLANTIC

9

Avalon

OCEAN

GARDEN STATE
PKY (TOLL)

Intracoastal
Waterway

47

Stone Harbor

Delaware
Bay

147

HEREFORD INLET
LIGHTHOUSE

North Wildwood

Wildwood

BOARDWALK

Cape May
Point State
Park

Wildwood Crest

CAPE MAY-
LEWES FERRY

Cape
May
Point

Cape May

CAPE MAY
LIGHTHOUSE

THE JERSEY SHORE
(SOUTH)

0   4 mi

0   4 km

Though New Jersey's native Lenape Indians spent time at the shore, the region didn't start becoming today's seaside resort until the 1850s, when railways bridged the gap between cities and beaches. At the same time, religious groups were establishing summer camps along the coast. The spiritual roots of places like Ocean City and Ocean Grove are evident along today's downtown streets, which don't allow liquor sales.

The Jersey Shore isn't *all* sun and games. Over the years, hundreds of shipwrecks have occurred off its coast; and in 1916, one of history's worst shark attacks took place in its waters. The Shore made news in the 1980s, when hospital-discarded hypodermic needles began washing up along its beaches. And more recently a local poll concluded that many people find the shore unfriendly (most people citing the "Jersey" attitude as the problem).

The Shore is a big place, and every New Jerseyan knows that a shore town or city can say a lot about you. While partiers head to Seaside Heights, Wildwood, and Belmar, families frequent Point Pleasant Beach and Ocean City. Couples tend to visit Spring Lake and Cape May, offering the best selection of bed-and-breakfasts statewide. Live music lovers make the drive to Asbury Park, and anyone preferring ritzy clubs and a little luxe (not to mention gambling) head to Atlantic City. New Yorker's stick to the Northern Shore while Philadelphians head to the Cape; the two meet up somewhere along Long Beach Island.

The best boardwalks—those with rides, souvenir shops, and deep-fried funnel cake—are in Point Pleasant, Seaside Heights, Atlantic City, Ocean City, and Wildwood; most towns without destination walkways, however, offer plenty of recreational activities to keep you occupied.

Remember, you don't have to be born in New Jersey to enjoy the Shore. Some locals may roll their eyes at weekenders "clogging" the beaches and stealing parking spots, but the shore belongs to everyone. So come Memorial Day, why not join the masses, heed the call, and head down the Shore? It's a bona fide Jersey experience.

PLANNING YOUR TIME

The Shore includes dozens of towns and cities with varying personalities. It's not a place you can, or should try to, cover in one visit. Most travelers stick to a particular town or region, though you may want to drive along the coast visiting highlights over the course of a week. One thing about the shore: It's versatile. It makes a perfect day trip, weekend escape, or seasonal excursion. But if your time is limited—say a day or weekend—choose a section near where you begin.

If arriving from New York City, stick to the Northern Shore or Barnegat Peninsula. Sandy Hook makes a good car-free day trip: It's accessible by ferry from Manhattan (summer only), and from there a bus will bring you to various peninsula points. For those traveling by car, continue the day with a coastal drive from Sea Bright to Spring Lake, a good place to stop if you're planning an overnight trip. Since prices at Spring Lake's bed-and-breakfasts can be steep during high season, consider backtracking to Ocean Grove for more affordable rates. On day 2, continue down the coast to Point Pleasant Beach for a stroll on family-friendly Jenkinson's Boardwalk. Or, for something a bit wilder, head into Seaside Heights for an afternoon at Breakwater Beach water park followed by a round of miniature golf and some wonderful people watching. The Garden State Parkway offers a quick return route to New York City.

From Philadelphia you'll get the most out of a day or weekend trip to the Cape or Long Beach Island. Cape May is a great spot for daytrippers. Enjoy breakfast in the city's historic district or at one of the beachfront eateries, then visit the Washington Mall Information Booth for details on the day's events and seats on one of the afternoon tours. Peruse the nearby shops, stroll along the Promenade, or admire the Victorian architecture before returning for your afternoon excursion. Following the tour you have a couple options: drive to Sunset Beach and search for Cape May diamonds before visiting nearby Cape May Lighthouse, or travel Ocean Drive north to Wildwood's boardwalk for pizza slices and people watching. Extend your day trip into a weekend and you can do it all. It's worth it just to spend a night in one of Cape May's several dozen Victorian B&Bs.

Many Jersey Shore establishments are shuttered in the off-season (Oct.–Apr.). For year-round Shore attractions, your best bets are Atlantic City and Cape May. With casinos, nightlife, shopping, and fine restaurants, it's easy to spend a weekend in Atlantic City without ever leaving, but if you're going a bit stir-crazy, head onto the mainland for tastings at one of the nearby wineries. As in summer, Cape May offers trolley tours and events throughout the Christmas holiday season. January and February are both quiet months, but things tend to pick up again come March.

During the height of summer many Shore accommodations require a 2–3 night minimum stay, usually on weekends. If possible, it's best to plan an overnight trip mid-week—accommodations are at their cheapest Tuesday–Thursday evenings. Take note that many dining establishments, especially along boardwalks, are cash-only.

Most Shore towns, including Belmar, Bradley Beach, Point Pleasant Beach, Beach Haven, Ocean City, Sea Isle, and the Wildwoods, offer weekly and seasonal rentals of homes, flats, and apartments, and local real estate agents tend to specialize in summer tourism (although many places are available for rent year-round, and the off-season is a *steal*). You can also go to New Jersey's http://craigslist.org and click on Jersey Shore housing for rental listings. The best time to search for your summer rental is January–March, when the selection is at it's best. Shore rentals go quickly.

Take note: Shore sand gets extremely hot during summer and can be unbearable to walk on without shoes. Invest in flip-flops.

INFORMATION AND SERVICES
Beach Tags
Most New Jersey beaches (Atlantic City and Wildwood are exceptions) require the use of beach tags Memorial Day–Labor Day. Daily costs range from $5–7 depending on the town. If you're planning a longer stay, it makes sense to purchase a weekly or seasonal pass, which will save you significant cash. Tags can usually be purchased at beachfront kiosks or by employees stationed at beach entryways. If there's no one around to collect your fee, it doesn't mean you're off the hook. Many beaches employ taggers to trudge up and down the sand checking tags as they go. You can try and feign sleep or run for a quick ocean dip when you see them approaching, but FYI—they're on to you, and will return at some point to see you cough up that cash. Yeah, it's a nuisance, but the money goes towards restoring the beaches for our future use. You can't argue with that. Still don't want to pay? Wait until after 5 P.M. when the lifeguards go off duty. You'll avoid the sun's stinging rays *and* the collection agency.

Since they're different from town to town and their designs are updated annually, New Jersey beach tags have become popular collectibles. You may think twice before tossing yours in the trash.

Visitors Centers
The Shore's only two welcome centers are located within the region's southern stretch. The **Atlantic City Welcome Center** (Atlantic City Expressway Mile Marker 3.5, Pleasantville, 609/383-2727) is situated along the Atlantic City Expressway right at the city's entry, and the Cape's **Ocean View Tourist Welcome Center** (Garden State Parkway Mile Marker 18.3 N/S, 609/624-0918) sits along the Garden State Parkway west of Sea Isle City. Both centers provide brochures, maps, and various pamphlets highlighting the local and surrounding regions.

Most New Jersey, Pennsylvania, and New York welcome centers provide information on the Jersey Shore. If you're already in the area and needing additional information, contact the local chamber of commerce.

Parking
Weekend parking during July and August is often a nightmare, especially in towns with

boardwalks. Private lots exist most places, but prices are steep ($10–20). It's best to reach your destination early, secure a parking spot away from the action (this limits the hunt), and stay put for a while. Weekdays aren't as bad, but if you plan on parking within easy walking distance to the shops or the beach, bring plenty of quarters—meters are the norm.

GETTING THERE AND AROUND

There are numerous ways to reach the Shore, depending on the town or city you're visiting. **NJ Transit's** (www.njtransit.com, 800/772-3606) North Jersey Coast Line runs trains daily from New York City as far south as Bay Head, with stops in Long Branch, Asbury Park, Bradley Beach, Belmar, Spring Lake, Manasquan, and Point Pleasant Beach. **SeaStreak** (732/872-2600 or 800/262-8743, www.seastreak.com) runs a daily commuter ferry from New York City to the Northern Shore's Highlands, and a daily summer ferry from Manhattan to Sandy Hook Gateway National Recreation Area.

Charter and bus tours from both New York City and Philadelphia are popular ways to reach Atlantic City, though Philly visitors can also catch NJ Transit's (www.njtransit.com) direct Atlantic City Line (ACL) from 30th Street Station. New Jersey residents can board the ACL at South Jersey's Lindenwold Station (901 Berlin Rd.). New York City's proposed Atlantic City Express Service (ACES) will operate between Penn Station and Atlantic City with one stop in Newark. As of this writing the plan is still undergoing review. Another way to reach the region is to fly. **Atlantic City International Airport** (609/645-7895, www .acairport.com) is a hub for **Spirit Airlines** (www.spiritair.com), which flies out of places such as Las Vegas and Florida. To reach the Cape without cross-state traffic, catch the **Cape May–Lewes Ferry** (800/643-3779, www .capemaylewesferry.com) in Lewes, Delaware. You'll be dropped off—car and all—just outside Cape May city.

If driving from North Jersey, the Garden State Parkway (a toll road) connects New York City and New York State, along with New Jersey's Gateway Region, to all of New Jersey's shore towns, traveling parallel to the state's eastern coastline straight through to Cape May. Traffic can get heavy during rush hour and summer weekends (especially Friday evenings), but otherwise it's a fairly no-nonsense route.

Another option from New York and North Jersey is Route 9 South (beginning as Rte. 1-9 in the Gateway Region). The road extends west of the Parkway until the Barnegat Bay region, where the two roads intersect. From here, Route 9 hugs the shoreline and remains there, for the most part, until the Cape region, when it once again crosses with the parkway.

The Atlantic City Expressway (accessible via Rte. 42) is the most straightforward route to Atlantic City and the Garden State Parkway for anyone arriving from Philadelphia, although the various tolls can add up. To reach towns along the Cape, a good option is Route 42 to Route 55, which leads into Route 47—a direct road into Wildwood. It's more scenic than the Parkway, though with only one lane heading each direction, traffic can easily back up. For Ocean City, take Route 49 west from Route 55.

Because of the large number of barrier islands and inlets, it's impossible to drive a straight north-south route along the Jersey Shore, although it is possible to explore the region in clusters. Route 36 travels east from the Highlands toward Sandy Hook and Sea Bright, turning south into Long Branch where it connects with local roads straight through to Manasquan. From here you can hop on Route 35 South and continue through Point Pleasant Beach and Seaside Heights straight into Island Beach State Park, where things get tricky. Although you can see Long Beach Island's Barnegat Lighthouse from Island Beach's southern tip, reaching it is not so easy. You have to backtrack to Seaside Heights and take Route 37 West to either Route 9 or the Garden State Parkway, traveling south to connect with Route 72 East, which will bring you to the Causeway Bridge connecting LBI to the mainland. The whole trip can take about an hour, but unless you have a boat it's the only way to do it. Scenic Ocean Drive connects greater Atlantic City with the southern Shore's Cape. It's a straight route with several toll bridges and stifling speed limits, but it's worth the ride. The drive is actually a series of local roads with various names, but it's instinctively easy to navigate. If you find yourself lost (all the better), don't hesitate to ask directions. Really, it's a straight shot.

The Northern Shore

Stretching from Sandy Hook's northern tip south to Manasquan, New Jersey's Northern Shore is a conglomeration of stately mansions, recovering (and recovered) cities, live-music venues, party bars, religious retreats, and romantic B&Bs. A decidedly New York and North Jersey hangout, this is where you'll find some of the Shore's best clubs and surfing locales, along with some excellent shopping opportunities. Beach erosion has reduced the size of the northernmost beaches, leading to the establishment of private beach clubs from Sea Bright (south of Sandy Hook) straight through to Long Branch. Further south, lakes and inlets separate the beach towns and lend postcard views. The Northern Shore is wider than much of the Jersey coast, creating a blend of beach town and residential suburb that continues straight through to the Point Pleasant Canal.

Information and Services
The free *Upstage* magazine (www.upstage magazine.com) provides local show listings and entertainment news for Jersey's Northern Shore. Look for it in stores.

For Northern Shore beach house weekly and seasonal rentals try **Diane Turton, Realtors** (www.dianeturton.com), with locations in Sea Bright, Ocean Grove, Avon-by-the-Sea, and Spring Lake, or **The Mary Holder Agency** (www.maryholder.com), in Bradley Beach, Sea Girt, and Manasquan.

Getting There and Around
NJ Transit's **North Jersey Coast Line** leaves from New York's Penn Station, Hoboken Terminal, and Newark's Penn Station, stopping in Long Branch, Asbury Park, Bradley Beach,

Belmar, Spring Lake, and Manasquan before continuing on to the Barnegat Peninsula.

◖ SANDY HOOK AND THE HIGHLANDS
On the upper portion of a barrier split protruding 11.2 miles north from the city of Long Branch sits seven-mile Sandy Hook Peninsula. Often mistaken as a town, Sandy Hook is actually part of the greater 26,000-acre New Jersey–New York **Gateway National Recreation Area;** a 1,665-acre natural formation of salt marshes, coves, forest, and beaches dividing Raritan Bay from the Atlantic Ocean. In 1974 Sandy Hook's southern portion—already a state park—joined with its northern half, home to a decommissioned U.S. defensive fort, and the two became part of the vast recreation facility.

There's plenty to do in Sandy Hook. Beaches on both the ocean and bay sides offer opportunities for swimming, sunning, birding, and water sports, and a multiuse trail perfect for walkers, runners, cyclists, and skaters runs the peninsula's entire length. Sandy Hook's North Beach offers a backdrop of the Manhattan skyline, and just south of it stands the remains of the former fort and military battery. A mile inland is the country's oldest continuously operating lighthouse, and farther south, the Atlantic Coast's highest density of holly forest, along with the state's only clothing-optional beach.

Most visitors combine a trip to Sandy Hook with one to the nearby Highlands, a seafaring town located on New Jersey's mainland, just over the Highlands Bridge. It's a natural pairing—west of the Sandy Hook Peninsula, the Highlands look like a European city rising

BENNIES VERSUS SHOOBIES

So you haven't spent every summer day since birth at the Shore, your folks didn't inherit a beach home from their parents, you don't recognize your seasonal neighbors or the people who own the upstairs flat, and you've never worked on the boards. You're obviously not a local — so which are you, a benny or a shoobie?

"Benny" is the name adopted for day-trippers along New Jersey's northern coast — an acronym for those arriving from the Great Northeast. The exact origin is unclear, but the word is a possible stand-in for "Bayonne, Eliza-beth, and Newark," or even "Bergen, Essex, and New York." Along New Jersey's Cape and southern coast, "shoobie" is the designation of choice, a name based on the day travelers who used to arrive down the Shore with their lunches secured firmly in shoeboxes. Although both terms may be taken as derogatory, they're often viewed lightheartedly — in Sea Isle City there's even a restaurant named Shoobies. Still, if you'd rather not be mistaken for either, wear the sunscreen, lose the socks, and don't spend an hour on your 'do before hitting the sticky, salty air.

from the hillside, beckoning visitors. Besides, this is where you'll find the area's B&Bs, along with a few wonderful dining choices.

Sights

Sandy Hook hosts the majority of local attractions, though the Highlands host a magnificent twin lighthouse that's worth seeing.

In service since 1764, **Sandy Hook Lighthouse** (Gateway National Recreation Area) is the oldest operating lighthouse in the United States. It is also one of New Jersey's smaller lighthouses, a 103-foot octagonal tower positioned more than a mile inland from Sandy Hook's northern tip. Free tours are conducted every half hour by the New Jersey Lighthouse Society, weekends noon–4:30 P.M. April–November. The lighthouse is also open during New Jersey's annual October Lighthouse Challenge, but if you plan to climb it, get here early (or late). Lines at this lighthouse are particularly long.

On Sandy Hook's northern half stand the remains of **Fort Hancock,** a U.S. coastal fort built to protect New York Harbor. Army personnel testing Sandy Hook Proving Ground's military artillery resided here. There was also a hospital, a school, a bakery, and a bowling alley. When Nike missiles, and later intercontinental missiles, replaced batteries fortified with disappearing guns, Fort Hancock was

declared surplus, and by 1975 it was all but abandoned. Today, there's an ongoing battle between preservationists and environmentalists to determine the future of these structures. Should they be restored, or should the land be returned to its natural state? Several of the buildings are currently occupied for research and educational purposes. Nearby still stand the decayed and weather-torn remnants of the old battery defenses.

Visitors can learn more about Fort Hancock's past by stopping by **Fort Hancock History House,** a restored 1898 lieutenant's residence situated along the bayside **Officer's Row.** The house is open weekends 1–5 P.M. and hosts a "Christmas during World War II" celebration each December. To find out more, or for information on the seasonal museum and bookstore located nearby, contact the Sandy Hook Visitor Center (732/872-5970).

At the north end of Officer's Row sits the 20-inch **Rodman Gun,** a Sandy Hook landmark and the largest smooth-bore muzzle-loader ever made.

Sandy Hook is considered one of New Jersey's best birding spots, with over 340 bird species living or migrating through annually, including flycatchers, buntings, loons, and grebes, and rarities like the swallow-tailed kite and Townsend's warbler. New Jersey's Audubon Society established the **Sandy Hook Bird Observatory**

(20 Hartshorne Dr., 732/872-2500, Tues.–Sat. 10 A.M.–5 P.M., Sun. 10 A.M.–3 P.M. Sept.–June, Tues.–Fri. 10 A.M.–5 P.M., Sat. 10 A.M.–3 P.M., closed Sun. July–Aug.) in 2001 to provide information on area birding spots and recent bird sightings. The center also hosts a small bookstore and gift shop.

Topping the Highlands' hillside 200 feet above sea level and the Raritan Bay are the **Twin Lights of Navesink** (Lighthouse Rd., Highlands, 732/872-1814, http://twin-lights .org), two turreted brownstone lighthouses connected by a long low-lying base. Not your typical tall and narrow structures, the Twin Lights look pretty ordinary when approached from the parking lot. To get their full effect, walk around front. It's also where you'll have the best view (without entering the lighthouse) of Sandy Hook and the sea below, and on a clear day, Manhattan. Built in 1862, the twin lights—one blinking and one stationary—helped distinguish the area for sailors. Both lights were decommissioned in 1949, although the north tower received a commemorative light in 1962. Self-guided north tower tours are allowed daily 10 A.M.–5 P.M. Memorial Day–Labor Day, and Wednesday–Sunday 10 A.M.–5 P.M. the remainder of the year. Admission is free. The south tower is open during the state's annual Lighthouse Challenge in October.

Beaches

Sandy Hook has miles of ocean beaches open to swimmers and sunbathers. The best swimming spots include the south beaches near Areas C and D, and **North Beach,** where wave-jumping comes with a Manhattan backdrop and a view of airplanes descending into JFK Airport. One of New Jersey's best-known beaches is also located nearby: Just south of the Hook's ocean midway, **Gunnison Beach** is the state's only clothing-optional beach. And just so you don't stumble across it unexpectedly, a warning sign reading BEYOND THIS POINT YOU MAY ENCOUNTER NUDE SUNBATHERS offers a heads-up.

Sandy Hook's beaches are open to the public all year, although there's a $10-per-vehicle parking fee (10 A.M.–4 P.M.) to enjoy them during summer months.

Sports and Recreation

The one-mile **Old Dune Trail,** beginning at Area D near the visitor center, offers a nice area overview, meandering near the coast through a densely populated 200-year-old holly forest. Before beginning, stop by the visitor center for an information packet describing possible flora sightings. A six-mile paved multiuse path, opened in 2004, runs the length of the peninsula. It's flat and easy to use, although wind exposure can be a nuisance.

Surf fishing is a popular activity along the Hook's Atlantic side, and a beach dedicated to the sport lies just north of Area D. Proper licensing is required. Windsurfing, kayaking, and sailing can all be enjoyed bayside, where you'll find a couple of small coves.

Accommodations

Bring your pooch for a stay at the Highlands' **SeaScape Manor B&B** (3 Grand Tour, Highlands, 732/291-8467, www.seascape manorbb.com, $119–195), with four lovely guest rooms all with private baths. The inn serves a complimentary gourmet breakfast in the dining room or seasonally on the outdoor deck, but you can also request it in-room. Stays include free use of SeaScape's beach tags.

Housed in a 1910 brick Victorian, the **Grand Lady by the Sea** (254 Rte. 36, Highlands, 732/708-1900 or 877/306-2161, www.grand ladybythesea.com, $139–249) offers six rooms, most with private baths, a few with ocean views, and all with complimentary breakfast. The inn has been renovated with original wood moldings and pocket doors, and there are subtle antique touches throughout. Perks include rental bikes and organic coffee.

Food and Entertainment

Sandy Hook's only dining establishment is located above the refreshment stand next to the visitor center. The **Sea Gull's Nest** (Area D, Hartshorne Dr., 732/872-0025, dawn–dusk summer, $6.50–10) serves casual

American fare on an outdoor deck overlooking the ocean. In addition to a full bar, the Nest closes each day with a recorded rendition of "God Bless America."

Just south of Sandy Hook is Sea Bright's **Donovan's Reef** (1171 Ocean Ave., 732/842-6789, www.donovansreefseabright.com), an area institution since 1976. Rumor has it that condos are moving in, and 2008 may be Donovan's last year. Here's hoping they're still slinging drinks as you read this. Donovan's attracts both Gen Y and Gen Xers, who gather at the outdoor tiki bar for live music and dancing, spilling over onto the establishment's private beach. An on-site grill selling burgers ($5.50) and shrimp-in-the-basket ($8.75) helps keep inevitable drunken antics at bay.

Located within a restored 100-year-old Highlands' bayside inn, popular **Doris & Ed's** (348 Shore Dr., Highlands, 732/872-1565, www.dorisandeds.com, Wed.–Fri. 5–10 P.M., Sat. 5–11 P.M., Sun. 3–10 P.M. Sept.–June, Tues.–Fri. 5–10 P.M., Sat. 5–11 P.M., Sun. 3–10 P.M. July–Aug., closed Mon. year-round, $30–50) specializes in fresh seafood and a selection of quality meat dishes—including a $68 Kobe beef special—along with more than 300 wines to choose from.

Another beloved seafood establishment, family-owned **Bahrs Landing Restaurant** (2 Bay Ave., Highlands, 732/872-1245, www.bahrs.com, Mon.–Thurs. 11:30 A.M.–10 P.M., Fri.–Sat. 11:30 A.M.–10:30 P.M., Sun. 11:30 A.M.–9 P.M. summer, hours vary slightly the rest of the year, $17–30) has been in business since 1917. Head indoors for fine dining, outdoors for kid-friendly chuckwagon-style meals and waterfront views.

Information and Services

Housed in a former 1894 U.S. Lifesaving Station, **Sandy Hook Visitor Center** (732/872-5970, daily 10 A.M.–5 P.M.) is located in Area D, two miles north of the park entrance. There's a bookstore, exhibits, and public restrooms on the premises, and a refreshment stand open April–October. Alcohol is allowed within park boundaries—but no glass containers.

Getting There and Around

SeaStreak (732/872-2600 or 800/262-8743, www.seastreak.com) and **New York Waterway** (800/533-3779, www.nywaterway.com) operate 30-minute Beach Excursion ferries (approx. $43 adult, $20 child round-trip) from New York City to Sandy Hook and back, daily throughout summer. A free shuttle for ferry riders operates from Area D to designated stops throughout the park, though you can also bring your bike aboard the ferry ($3 one way) and use it for commuting once you arrive. The company also runs ferries between the Highlands (Conner's Ferry Landing) and New York City's Wall Street or 34th Street daily year-round (6 A.M.–10 P.M.), with a limited weekend schedule. Round-trip fares are $43 adult (no child fare is offered) during peak weekday hours (before 9:30 A.M.), and $35 adult, $19 child on weekends.

A daily shuttle bus ($1, free for ferry passengers) operates around Sandy Hook during summer months, stopping at beaches and park sites throughout the peninsula, including Fort Hancock Museum, North Beach, and Gunnison Beach.

LONG BRANCH

What began as an elitist gambling resort and became a vacationing spot for big money men like railroad financier Jay Gould and seven U.S. presidents, including Ulysses S. Grant, Rutherford B. Hayes, and James A. Garfield, has emerged from a period of economic blight, finally regaining its niche as an upscale resort community. Recently the "Friendly City" has wiped out much of its waterfront property, rebuilding from the ground up (a preservationist's nightmare) with money invested by state and federal agencies. High-rises and condos now occupy prime beachfront real estate. Signs of "progress" are everywhere along the water, but take Broadway west and the city's struggling past is evident. Wild West legends Annie Oakley and Buffalo Bill both spent time in the city, as did actor Edwin Booth (of Washington, D.C.'s Booth Theatre) and the Gould and Astor families, but with so much reinvention, finding a hint of their history is difficult. Long Branch is about an hour's drive from New York City.

Sights

Long Branch's noncommercial waterfront walkway offers unbeatable views, but only because it's east of the city's recent construction boom. Although it's at street level, the walkway rises about six feet above the sand, and there's a dedicated bike path running beside it. Along the walkway is a monument honoring 20th U.S. President James A. Garfield, who died in Long Branch after retiring here to recuperate from an assassination attempt in Washington, D.C.

Built in 1881 as a house of worship for visiting U.S. Presidents, St. James Historic Chapel—now known as the **Church of Presidents**—is home to the **Long Branch Historical Museum** (1260 Ocean Ave., 732/229-0600, www.churchofthepresidents .org), and is located directly across the street from where James A. Garfield died. Due to the church's deteriorating condition, the museum's collection—which includes Ulysses S. Grant's gun cabinet and game table, and the church's original pipe organ—was removed in 1999. Plans are currently underway to restore the church and reopen it to the public.

Pier Village (732/528-8509, www.pier village.com), a waterfront residential and retail complex housing over 30 boutique stores and restaurants, began accepting tenants in 2005. Stores include local surf shop **Aloha Grove** (732/263-0100, www.alohagrove.com), **Atlantic Books** (732/571-4300), and craft art gallery **Arrivée** (732/222-9366, www.arrivee gallery.com).

In nearby Oceanport, **Monmouth Park Racetrack** (Oceanport Ave., 732/222-5100, www.monmouthpark.com, 11:30 A.M.–5 P.M., $2 adult, child free) features live thoroughbred horse racing throughout summer and into the shoulder seasons. The racetrack is a favorite TV filming locale, with cameos in both *The Sopranos* and *Law & Order*. ATMs and a gift shop are located on the first floor, and the track hosts several restaurants and concession stands.

Beaches

Much of Long Branch's oceanfront is considered private, so for sunbathing and body boarding head to **Seven Presidents Oceanfront Park** (Ocean Ave. at Joline Ave., 732/229-7025 or 732/229-0924 in summer, $6), also featuring volleyball courts and a skateboard park. Long Branch hosts a handful of other public beaches, including North Bath Avenue, West End Avenue, and Morris Avenue, all of which have public restrooms. The city's surfing beach is at Matilda Terrace. For a full list of Long Branch public-access beaches, call the **Greater Long Branch Chamber of Commerce** at 732/571-1833.

Daily beach tags cost $5 adult, $3 age 13–17, and 12 and under free. A season pass is $35 adult, $30 child age 13–17.

Accommodations

Located in the city's West End district near Monmouth Park Racetrack is the 12-room **Cedars and Beeches Bed & Breakfast** (247 Cedar Ave., 800/323-5655, www.cedarsand beeches.com, $160–250), a spacious Victorian with a wraparound covered porch perfect for escaping summer humidity. A bit of a hike from the beach, it is best suited for business travelers (high-speed Internet is available) and those looking to rejuvenate.

The upscale **Ocean Place Resort & Spa** (1 Ocean Blvd., 800/411-6493, www.ocean placeresort.com, $299–399) occupies prime waterfront property—and has its own private beach—but that doesn't mean you're required to take an ocean dip. With both an indoor and outdoor pool and an on-site spa, you've got plenty of luxuries to choose from. Rooms have private balconies (some with superb ocean views) and for an extra $150 your pet can come along too. There's also a restaurant, lounge, and seasonal low-carb café on-site.

Food and Nightlife

Tucked behind Long Branch's newer development, **Rooney's Oceanfront Restaurant** (100 Ocean Ave., 732/870-1200, www .rooneysocean.com, Mon.–Thurs. and Sun.

11:30 A.M.–10 P.M., Fri.–Sat. 11:30 A.M.–11:30 P.M., $16–45) is a gem worth finding. Its prime beachfront location offers sweeping ocean views, especially from the restaurant's bi-level outdoor deck. Standouts include Rooney's changing seafood specials and an expansive wine selection. Though attire varies, you'll probably want to forgo the shorts and flip-flops.

It may look like a dive, but **Brighton Bar** (121 Brighton Ave., 732/229-9676, www.cojackproductions.com) has been a favorite live music venue for over 20 years. The bar showcases New Jersey bands and national acts ranging from jazz to rock for the 18-and-older crowd. Weekday performances are $7, weekend shows $9.

Getting There and Around

Long Branch is located off Exit 105 of the Garden State Parkway.

NJ Transit's North Jersey Coast Line operates from New York Penn Station with a stop at **Long Branch Train Station** (3rd Ave. between North Bath Ave. and Morris Ave.), just north of the **Monmouth Medical Center.** The trip takes approximately 1.5 hours one-way, and off-peak round-trip fare is $20.50 adult, $10.25 child. The station is a hike from the beach, so bring along a bike for transport.

ASBURY PARK

The crumbling and abandoned buildings, graffitied facades, and an overall sense of desolation may have some people asking, "What's the allure?" But Asbury Park has one, and now it looks as though things may finally be turning this city's way. The queen of New Jersey's Shore during the first half of the 20th century, Asbury Park entered a downward spiral when the state's Garden State Parkway opened in the 1950s, paving a route to beaches further south. The city was soon taken over by motorcycles and music, but what business that brought in was damaged for good in the 1970s, when race riots split Asbury Park in two and the city was abandoned, almost completely.

Thankfully, years of neglect have left many of Asbury Park's architecturally grand structures untouched, but whether this will hold true with the onslaught of new development is another story. Palace Amusements succumbed to the wrecking ball in 2004, and the Baronet Theatre, Upstage Club (where Springsteen *really* got his start), and even the Stone Pony have all been threatened in the name of progress.

It still holds true that Asbury has seen better days, but rarely does a city fight such a heartfelt battle to bring those days back. True, the city has been "up and coming" for a while, but results are finally showing. A notable gay community has breathed new life into Asbury Park, introducing shops and restaurants, a hotel and nightclub, and an annual gay pride parade. And along Cookman Avenue, storefronts are being filled by retro boutiques, coffeehouses, and art galleries. The boardwalk has seen endless construction through 2008, including brand-new shops, a makeover for the casino arcade and its carousel house, and even a miniature golf course.

Ocean Avenue remains riddled with potholes, and crime does occur, but there are plenty of reasons to visit Asbury Park. Not to linger on the boards after dark, mind you, but for the excellent restaurants, unique shopping ops, stunning architecture, the beach, history, art…and surely, the music.

Sights

In 2004 Asbury Park's new mile-long million-dollar **boardwalk** debuted as part of the city's new look, and in 2008 a whole slew of recently constructed shops were set to open, giving strollers plenty to explore between Convention Hall and the casino, connecting the walkway to Ocean Grove's. You won't be mistaking these boards for Seaside Heights or Wildwood any time soon, but you wouldn't want to. It's rare to have such a pleasant stretch of beachfront property practically to yourself, and it won't last long. Go on: take a stroll, ride your bike, peruse the shops, play a round of miniature golf (when was the last time you

ASBURY'S CLOWN

Tillie the clown is one of New Jersey's most iconic faces. Two nearly identical images, each 200 feet high, 13 feet wide, both strewn with neon tubes and sporting Cheshire-cat grins, prominently adorned Asbury Park's Palace Amusements' exterior, their blue eyes watching over residents and visitors since 1956. Over the years Tillie and Asbury Park became synonymous. He was featured in movies and TV shows such as *The Sopranos* and appeared in Springsteen publicity shots and on concert merchandise.

Tillie's life began through the artful hand of Leslie "Worth" Thomas, a graphic design artist hired by Asbury Park's Central Amusement Corporation to provide the Palace with a fun house feel. Thomas added a unique touch by painting the names of rides like Olympic Bob's and Tunnel of Love in curvaceous letters on the Palace walls. But while Tillie's faces came from his brush, they didn't come directly from Thomas's imagination.

Tillie's origin can be traced back to 1897, when a smiling caricature known as the Steeplechase Fun Face decorated Coney Island's Steeplechase Park Pavilion of Fun. Both the park and the fun face were destroyed by fire in 1907, but Steeplechase was rebuilt, and for the next four decades a Fun Face version appeared on everything from entry tickets to advertisements, although each portrayal was slightly different from the last. Eventually standardized in the 1940s, Fun Face disappeared when the park was demolished in 1964. But the faces of Steeplechase live on in Tillie. Even his name derives from ancestral roots: Tillie is short for George C. Tiylou, Steeplechase's founding father.

Palace life began for Tillie just as Asbury Park was reaching its end as a well-known vacation venue. Families started heading south to beach towns such as Beach Haven and Wildwood, and a new crowd began moving in. By the 1970s the bikers, street gangs, and music scene Springsteen immortalized in his lyrics had found a home in Asbury Park. But nothing seemed able to save the Palace, which soon fell like much of the city into disrepair. On November 27, 1988, the Palace closed its doors without warning, and Tillie's neon lights shone for the last time.

For almost a decade the Palace and Tillie stood untouched and seemingly forgotten, until the *Asbury Park Press* reported the building was in danger of collapsing and demolition was imminent. Within a day, thepreservation group **Save Tillie** (www.savetillie.com) was formed. Their original goal was to save at least one Tillie painting, removing it from the Palace intact and relocating it to another area of the city. Save Tillie has since grown into a nonprofit with hundreds of members and support from many local musicians, including Bruce. The group has expanded their efforts to preserving Asbury Park's unique architecture and history, like the Stone Pony, most famously associated with Springsteen.

In June 2004, Palace Amusements was demolished, but not before the group's volunteers saved Tillie. Unfortunately, the Palace property's current owners, Asbury Partners, have housed him in a poorly constructed leaky shed. Whether Tillie will have a future remains uncertain, but Save Tillie members are not giving up. For ways you can help save Tillie and Asbury Park's past, visit the group's website. And for a glimpse of Tillie in the meantime, check out Asbury Park's Wonder Bar: That crazy clown is still smilin' down.

heard *that* in Asbury?). Do it now, before you have to wait in line.

It's unclear what will happen to fortuneteller Madame Marie's little blue boardwalk shack now that she has passed away. The seer became famous when she appeared in the lyrics of Springsteen's song, "Fourth of July, Asbury Park (Sandy)," and her **Temple of Knowledge** (732/775-5327) has long been a photo-op favorite. When Marie (her real name was Marie Castello) died in late June 2008 at age 93, the city's Convention Hall lowered its flag to half-staff. Most recently Castello's daughter and daughter-in-law have been operating the temple. Whether they'll continue sharing fortunes without the matriarch, we'll have to wait and see.

Asbury Park's new and improved carousel house

Asbury Park is the birthplace of Jersey Shore music, and it's well known that this movement's main purveyor is none other than Brother Bruce. The **Asbury Park Public Library** (500 1st Ave., 732/774-4221, www.asbury parklibrary.org, Mon.–Wed. 11 A.M.–8 P.M., Thurs.–Fri. 9 A.M.–5 P.M., Sat. noon–5 P.M., closed Sun.) houses what's considered to be the largest collection of Boss memorabilia, including songbooks, tour books, newspaper articles, and academic papers, in the world. Much of the early collection was a gift from long-running (and awesome) Springsteen fan magazine *Backstreets*. Because library staff is limited, it's recommended you call and make an appointment to access the material before showing up. A list of the collection's current holdings is available on the library website.

Newark native and *The Red Badge of Courage* author Stephan Crane moved to Asbury Park in the late 1880s following his father's death. Crane penned his first short story at 508 4th Avenue. Designated the **Stephen Crane House** (732/775-5682, http://asburyradio .com/Cranehouse.htm, call for hours), the home

now operates as a museum and performing arts space, hosting readings, plays, and movies.

Beaches

Asbury Park's daily beach tags cost $5 weekdays and weekends, age 12 and under free. A season pass costs $50. The city's beaches remain fairly deserted—you should have little trouble finding a place to lay your blanket. The best place to do so is in front of the boardwalk, between Convention Hall and the casino. The beach itself is lovely—a wide stretch of gleaming white sand—though for something a little livelier, walk through the casino to nearby Ocean Grove. A caveat: Their beaches are twice the price of Asbury's on weekends.

Shopping

Asbury's **Cookman Avenue,** the city's main street, is looking better than ever. A slew of new shops has moved in over the last few years, and while some favorites like Antic Hay Books (*sigh*) have closed their doors, the future shows tremendous promise. There are several antique stores to explore, as well as art galleries, clothing boutiques, and a shop selling retro kitchenware.

Wish You Were Here! (612 Cookman Ave., 732/774-1601, www.wishyouwerehereap.com) features a candy counter filled with goodies—chocolate-covered cherries, dark chocolate oozing with absinthe, and frosted cookies made to look like local icon Tillie the Clown—although its memorabilia collection is just as sweet. Pick up a miniature mechanical Ferris wheel or Asbury Park paintings by local watercolorist P. J. Carlino.

For hemp handbags, organic cotton T-shirts, and formaldehyde-free nail polish, stop by **Organic Style** (621 Cookman Ave., 732/775-1051, www.organicstyleshop.com). Afterward, swing over to **Crybaby Art Gallery** (717 Cookman Ave., 732/869-0606, www.crybaby artgallery.com) to browse cutting-edge works of pop, surrealist, and graffiti art.

Mike's Beach House (619 Cookman Ave., 732/988-6088, www.mikesbeachhouse.net) is the place to find Shore souvenirs like postcards, saltwater taffy, and custom wooden Asbury Park signs. Proprietors of the retro-fashion boutique **Allan & Suzi** (711 Cookman Ave., 732/988-7372) have dressed celebs including Robin Williams and the *Sex and the City* cast in their vintage finds. Stock includes Gucci, Prada, and Jimmy Choo shoes.

Tucked into the **Shoppes at the Arcade** in the former Woolworth Building, **Flying Saucers Retro Kitchenware** (658 Cookman Ave. Unit 13, 732/202-8848, www.flyingsaucers online.com) carries a fabulous selection of kitchen folk art, Fiesta ware, Kit-Cat Klocks, mixing bowls, and more. Also among the shops is the original (and operational) **Palace Amusement B&W Photo Booth.** You just *know* Bruce has been in there at some point.

Antique Emporium of Asbury Park (646 Cookman Ave., 732/774-8230, www.antique emporiumofasburypark.com) houses over 60 antique vendors, including the arts and crafts–era furniture of **Tristan's Antiques** (www .tristansantiques.com). The Antique Emporium supplies to B&Bs, stage designers, and major motion picture companies. The 5,000-square-foot **Studebakers–Antiques and Collectibles Mall** (1201 Main St., 732/776-5565) is home to 30 antique and collectible dealers, as well as the **Rumble Seat Tea Room,** an ideal spot to savor your kitchenware purchases and Civil War finds.

Up on the boardwalk, **Asbury Galleria** (3rd Ave. Boardwalk Pavilion, 732/869-9977, www.asburygalleria.com) features Jersey Shore books and photos by longtime local resident Milton Edelman. Asbury Park's urban surf shop **Lightly Salted** (3rd Ave. Boardwalk Pavilion, 732/776-8886, www.lightlysalted surf.blogspot.com) opened in August 2008. In addition to custom boards and alternative coastal art, expect a place to chill. I'm stoked about **Hot Sand** (5th Ave. Boardwalk Pavilion, 732/927-5475, www.hotsandap.com), the city's hands-on glass studio. In addition to workshops in glassblowing and glass fusing, Hot Sand offers studio rental, hosts events, and sells handmade glass works inspired by Asbury Park. For a boardwalk bike rental there's now **Brielle Cyclery** (5th Ave. Boardwalk Pavilion, 732/502-0077, www.briellecyclery.com), open daily throughout summer.

Entertainment and Nightlife

Opened in 1923, the beachfront's 3,600-seat **Convention Hall** is impressive—a red-brick art deco structure built by the architects responsible for New York City's Grand Central Terminal. Joined to it by the Grand Arcade extending over the boardwalk, the street-side 1930 **Paramount Theatre** is just as stunning. Both venues are listed on the National Register of Historic Places and host concerts, festivals, and conventions throughout the year. The Paramount Theatre is the acoustically superior of the two, and the Convention Hall is a bit more rugged, with no heat or air-conditioning. The latter has become a favorite rehearsal venue for Springsteen and the E Street Band. Fans who don't manage to score a ticket can simply set up on the sand below and listen to the show.

Made famous by the Boss, Asbury Park's **The Stone Pony** (913 Ocean Ave., 732/502-0600, www.thestonepony.com) didn't actually

© LAURA KINIRY

Asbury Park's historic Paramount Theatre and Convention Hall

open until 1974, a year after Bruce released *Born to Run*. The building was originally occupied by a restaurant called Mrs. Jays, later becoming the Magic Touch disco bar, which was abandoned by the time John P. "Jack" Roig and Robert "Butch" Pielka decided to open the Pony. In addition to its Springsteen association, the Stone Pony gets cred for its rockin' house band, the Asbury Jukes, often cited as one of the world's greatest bar bands. The band still performs here. See a show at the Pony—it's like bathing in rock and roll.

Live bands take stage at **The Saint** (601 Main St., 732/775-9144, www.thesaintnj .com, $7–15) 5–7 days a week. Since 1994, this 175-capacity 18-and-over club has been the place to see up-and-comers, including Jewel and Stereophonics. There are 20 brews on tap, and all-age weekend matinees. The Asbury Music Company, parent company of the Saint, presents annual awards recognizing the best local talent.

A long-running bowling alley that has been converted into one of the hippest, hottest, baddest clubs in town, **Asbury Lanes** (209 4th Ave., 732/776-6160, www.asburylanes.com, Wed.–Sat. 8 P.M.–2 A.M.) is worth a trip. Punk nights and some fabulous art shows, including a 2007–2008 exhibit of painted bowling pins, are held year-round, and the lanes are still in use. The club's past live shows have included a Burlesque Bikini Blowout, the Yard Dogs, and Big City Bombers. To enter the club is age 18, to drink age 21, unless noted otherwise.

One of New Jersey's largest gay clubs is situated on the bottom floor of the renovated Empress Hotel. **Paradise** (101 Asbury Ave., 732/988-6663, www.paradisenj.com, Wed.–Thurs. 4 P.M.–2 A.M., Sat.–Sun. noon–2 A.M.) features two dance floors, two stages, and an outdoor pool with a hanging disco ball. Poolside happy hour is held weekday afternoons throughout summer.

Accommodations

In keeping with the city's revitalization theme, Asbury Park's historic **Berkeley Oceanfront Hotel** (1401 Ocean Ave., 732/776-6700, www .berkeleyhotelnj.com, $83–137) has been completely renovated with a new lobby, stylish guest rooms, and poolside private cabanas and tiki bar. It's quite a change from the worn and weathered hotel that stood here before. Granted the building is still old, but the decor is fun and modern. There's even a pool table in the lobby.

Just south of Asbury Park, Ocean Grove offers dozens of B&B options.

Food

Sunset Landing (1215 Sunset Ave., 732/776-9732, daily 7 A.M.–2 P.M., $6–11) is an Asbury Park classic, a family-owned diner/surf shack that serves a killer breakfast and also rents out canoes for use on Deal Lake, where the eatery is located. Cookman Avenue's **Twisted Tree Cafe** (609 Cookman Ave., 732/775-2633) bakes and serves vegan cupcakes, breads, muffins, and more, alongside a vegetarian menu dotted with bean wraps ($8) and hummus sandwiches ($8). Replenish your tummy, then order yourself a chai latte and stay a while.

The Boardwalk's iconic Howard Johnson's structure has been renovated and now houses the **Salt Water Beach Café** (732/774-1400, www.saltwaterbeachcafenj.com, Sun.–Thurs. 11 A.M.–10 P.M., Fri.–Sat. 11 A.M.–11 P.M., $11–30), offering a selection of artisanal sandwiches and upscale entrées. Visitors can nosh on softshell crab or pulled-pork sandwiches while admiring the crashing waves.

Ocean Grove transplant **Moonstruck** (517 Lake Ave., 732/988-0123, www.moonstrucknj .com, Wed.–Thurs. and Sun. 5–10 P.M., Fri.–Sat. 5–11 P.M., closed Mon.–Tues., $15–33) has been luring Asbury Park crowds with its romantic terraces, exquisite Mediterranean fare, and awesome views since 2004. Housed in a refurbished three-story shore home, the restaurant features a main-floor cocktail lounge and two upper-level dining areas, both with wraparound porches overlooking Wesley Lake. Get here early—reservations aren't accepted.

Asbury's Main Street still has a ways to go, but a good start is **Bistro Olé** (230 Main St., 732/897-0048, www.bistroole.com, dinner Tues.–Thurs. and Sun. 5–10 P.M., Fri.–Sat. 5–11 P.M., closed Mon., $19–29), a colorful and boisterous BYO with a gregarious host and tasty Spanish-Portuguese dishes—like seared sea bass topped with pesto and breadcrumbs ($29)—galore. Seating is first come, first served.

Getting There and Around

Asbury Park is 40 miles south of Manhattan, just off Exit 102 southbound (100A northbound) of the Garden State Parkway. The **Asbury Park Train Station** is at the south end of Cookman Avenue, an easy stroll to downtown's shops and within reasonable walking distance to the boardwalk.

OCEAN GROVE

Founded in the late 19th century as a Methodist summer camp, "God's Square Mile" has remained successfully true to its roots. While strict blue laws—such as no driving on Sundays—have been lifted, others—like restricted Sunday-morning beach use—remain in effect. The Great Auditorium is the city's center, a popular religious revival venue surrounded by narrow streets, all packed by multi-story Stick Victorians in various states of repair. Across from the beach stand faded gingerbread clapboards, their long porches piled atop one another to utilize the ocean breezes. Just north of the auditorium are the canvas tents of Ocean Grove's original settlers. Each with a pitched roof and porch awning, they're still in use by seaside vacationers.

The Grove has been considered part of Neptune Township since the 1980s, but it retains its own downtown filled with ice cream stands and specialty shops. A noncommercial boardwalk runs along the beach, connecting with Asbury Park's boardwalk to the north. Affordable bed-and-breakfasts are scattered throughout town, many of them more like hostels or boarding hotels than boutique lodging. Patients released from an area mental hospital in the 1980s and gays migrating in from neighboring Asbury Park have added a whirlpool mix to local demographics—one that, by most accounts, nobody seems to mind.

Bed-and-breakfasts are scattered throughout Ocean Grove.

Sights

Connecting with Asbury Park's boardwalk to the north, the noncommercial Ocean Grove **boardwalk** is strictly for strolling.

Ocean Grove's centerpiece, the 6,500-seat **Great Auditorium** (21 Pilgrim Pathway, 732/775-0035 or 800/773-0097), is impossible to miss. This massive (almost as large as a football field) wood structure, built as a house of worship, hosts family-friendly shows such as the poodle-skirt-swaying Doo Wop Revue and acts like the Smothers Brothers, as well as religious services. Across the street is the **Auditorium Pavilion,** an open-air gazebo hosting book sales and a weekly church service.

Alongside the Great Auditorium is **Tent City,** over 100 canvas tents originally leased to Methodist church members—the Grove's founders—during the late 19th century. The tents are still owned by the Ocean Grove Camp Meeting Association, although you don't have to belong to the church to rent one. You do, however, have to sign your name to an extremely long waiting list—more than 20 years.

Many of the tents feature colorfully striped awnings perched above their entryways, and bicycles and beach chairs hang from their sides. Almost all have been added to over the years. Sneak a peek inside and you'll see they're just like other homes—quilt-covered beds, comfy couches, and plenty of knickknacks. You haven't seen Ocean Grove unless you've seen Tent City.

Beaches

Ocean Grove's daily beach tags are $7 weekdays, a whopping $12 weekends, under age 12 free. There are both weeklong ($35) and season ($70) passes available as well. On Sundays, beach use is restricted until noon. Fishing is allowed from beach jetties; the best times for fishing are 5 A.M.–7 A.M. and after 8 P.M.

Events

Ocean Grove Historical Society (732/774-1869, www.oceangrovehistory.org, Mon. and Wed.–Thurs. 10 A.M.–4 P.M., Fri.–Sat. 10 A.M.–5 P.M.) hosts numerous events year-round, including annual summer and

Christmas **House Tours,** and 90-minute **Historic District Walking Tours** (Wed. and Fri. 1 P.M., Sat. 11 A.M., June–mid-Sept.), which include visits to Tent City and the Great Auditorium. Tours begin in front of 50 Pitman Avenue, the Society museum.

Shopping

Take some time to peruse Main Street's shops, stopping off for an ice cream cone along the way.

Main Street is home to several collectibles shops, including the country-style **Favorite Things** (52 Main Ave., 732/774-0230, www.1800foragift.com). Housed in an old Victorian, the selection includes hand-painted furniture, period lace, and quilted bags. There's also an old-fashioned chocolate and candy counter for sweet-toothed passers-by. Year-round **Comfort Zone** (44-46 Main Ave., 732/869-9990, www.comfortzone-og.com) stocks aromatherapy candles, body lotions, and home accessories such as stained glass window hangings. Funky **Kitsch and Kaboodle** (76 Main Ave., 732/869-0950) features Burt's Bees lip balms alongside retro Barbies and vintage tableware. For all things Victorian, stop by **Gingerbreads Teas & Treasures** (49 Main Ave., 732/775-7900), also the place for Steiff stuffed animals and baby toys.

Located on the first floor of the Majestic Hotel, **Ocean Grove Surf Shop** (19 Main Ave., 732/869-1001, ogsurfshop.com) is a retro surf shop stocking clothing, boards, and accessories. Surf lessons are held during shop hours (daily 9 A.M.–7 P.M. summer). Call ahead to schedule, and check online for a 24-hour surf report.

Accommodations

The prettiest part of Ocean Grove—near the Great Auditorium—is also where you'll find many of the bed-and-breakfasts. Rooms tend to be small and lack modern amenities, although this is reflected in more affordable prices. Ocean Avenue establishments offer some of the best views, not to mention a cool ocean breeze.

One of Ocean Grove's newer B&Bs, the four-story **Henry Richard Inn** (16 Main Ave., 732/776-7346, www.henryrichardinn.com, $85–95) features single and double units with in-room sinks and a shared bath, along with two fully contained apartments. A full complimentary breakfast is served daily.

In addition to ocean breezes, the seasonal corner-lot **House by the Sea** (14 Ocean Ave., 732/774-4771, $85–135) offers a fabulous beachfront view from its front porch. There are no room telephones or TVs, and only a limited number of private baths. The living is simple but good.

Half a block away from the Great Auditorium is the 36-room **Manchester Inn** (25 Ocean Pathway, 732/775-0616, www.themanchester inn.com, $105–290), New Jersey's first solar-powered inn. This multistory white Victorian, once two separate buildings, has received accolades for its Murder Mystery Weekends, held in later spring and early fall. Many of the rooms rely on ocean air and ceiling fans for cooling, and a lengthy covered front porch with rocking chairs offers afternoon and evening relief. Although some bathrooms are shared, all rooms have their own sink. The inn offers half-day rates and free wireless Internet. Complimentary hot breakfast is served daily.

One of the town's smaller B&Bs, the eight-room **Carriage House** (18 Heck Ave., 732/998-9441, www.carriagehousenj.com, $125–180) occupies a renovated century-old Victorian along a quiet street. All the rooms feature a private bath, TV, and air-conditioning, and the larger ones have working fireplaces. This smoke-free inn is unable to accommodate kids.

An easy walk from the beach is **Lillagaard Hotel** (5 Abbot Ave., 732/998-1216, www .lillagaard.com, $120–175), an imposing 22-room Victorian with an English Countryside feel. Each room is uniquely designed with hand-painted murals, and there's a TV room, a library, and a dining room where complimentary breakfast is served. Air-conditioning comes with every room; private baths accompany most rooms.

With wraparound porches and sweeping

ocean views, the year-round Victorian **Ocean Plaza** (18 Ocean Pathway, 732/774-6552, www.ogplaza.com, $185–325) is a coveted establishment. Sixteen guest rooms and three suites each come equipped with modern amenities like TV and a VCR, central air, and private bathrooms—features that are hard to come by at the bulk of Ocean Grove B&Bs. A daily continental breakfast can be enjoyed from the second-story veranda during warmer months, offering fine people-watching opportunities below.

Food

The bulk of Ocean Grove's eateries are along Main Street, although several are scattered among the town's B&Bs. Most eateries around here tend to keep things casual, catering to the Shore appeal.

For breakfast try downtown's **Starving Artist at Days** (47 Olin St., 732/988-1007, Mon.–Sat. 8 A.M.–3 P.M., Sun. 8 A.M.–2 P.M., closed Wed., $6–12), also serving lunch throughout the week (except Wed.). The Artist dishes out theatrical entertainment, such as the musical *Godspell*, in its outdoor Victorian Garden.

The intimate **Raspberry Café** (60 Main Ave., 732/988-0071, Tues.–Thurs. 11 A.M.–7 P.M., Fri.–Sat. 11 A.M.–3 P.M. and 5–9 P.M., $8–25) offers a small lunch and dinner selection alongside a creative assortment of starters and salads. Sandwiches include an open-faced portobello with sautéed spinach ($8), and a three-cheese grilled cheese with tomato ($8).

Century-old **Nagles Apothecary Café** (43 Main St., 732/776-9797, daily 8:30 A.M.–9 P.M., closed Tues., $5–10) is a former pharmacy that has evolved into a classic American eatery complete with soda fountain and some of the best ice cream around (go for the peanut butter swirl). The café includes indoor and outdoor seating, and a take-out window that's popular even on rainy days.

On the Majestic Hotel's ground floor is the European-style **Bia,** a recently renovated and revamped 60-seat bistro serving a variety of light fare and innovative entrées, like jumbo scallops over lobster ravioli ($28) and filet mignon wrapped in smoked bacon ($34). Hours are daily noon–10 P.M. with brunch Sunday 11:30 A.M.–4 P.M. seasonally, although the inn also offers year-round dining on its 24-seat enclosed heated porch.

Getting There and Around

Ocean Grove is located just off Exit 100 of the Garden State Parkway. NJ Transit's **North Jersey Coast Line** stops in Asbury Park just across the lake from Ocean Grove.

BRADLEY BEACH

Just south of Ocean Grove is Bradley Beach, a pleasant borough founded by middle-class Philadelphians and New Yorkers in the late 19th century. Today, it's filled with one- and two-story colonials that look as though they've been passed down through generations. Thankfully, local zoning laws prevent any additional buildup. A couple of beachfront brick structures seem misplaced, but Bradley Beach is otherwise attractive, comfortable, and friendly. There are several fine Italian restaurants downtown, and a short stretch of Mexican shops and eateries catering to the borough's significant Latino population. A beachfront promenade hosts benches, gazebos, a few food stands, a miniature golf course, and boccie ball courts (4th Ave.), and bicycles are allowed on the walkway midnight–10 A.M. Memorial Day–Labor Day. Several Bradley Beach restaurants are open year-round.

Beaches

Daily beach tags cost $7 adult, free for those 13 and under. A season pass costs $65. Food and beverages are permitted on the beach, but no alcohol. Fishing is allowed on beach jetties at Lake Terrace, Park Place, Brinley Avenue, and 2nd Avenue. A one-mile beach stretch between Third and Fifth Avenues is reserved for surfers only. There are public restrooms at Newark, LaReine, Third, and Evergreen Avenues, and showers along the beach. The borough hosts a gazebo concert series at Fifth Avenue and the ocean (www.bradleybeachonline.com) evenings throughout summer.

Accommodations

Just steps from the beach, the three-story Victorian **Bradley Beach Inn** (900 Ocean Ave., 732/774-0414, www.thebradleybeachinn.com, $105–165) offers eight simple guest rooms, most with flower duvets, several with ocean views, and two with an extra full-size bed (for families). Some bathrooms are shared.

The **Sandcastle Inn** (204 3rd Ave., 732/774-2875, www.sandcastleinn.us, $130–270) offers six simple guest rooms and two suites, each with a private bath and wireless Internet access. While some rooms, like the bright Wildflowers room, include air-conditioning, others depend strictly on the sea breeze. Use of two beach tags, chairs, and a beach umbrella is complimentary.

Food

Always-bustling **La Nonna Piancone's Cafe** (800 Main St., 732/775-0906, www.piancone .com, Sun.–Thurs. 8 A.M.–7 P.M., Fri.–Sat. 8 A.M.–9 P.M., $12–29) recently changed ownership, revamping its interior with a classy new upstairs fit for live entertainment. Having been family-owned and operated for more than 50 years, patrons are in for a few changes, although the Mediterranean restaurant's reputation as grandma's substitute kitchen is expected to stick. La Nonna also houses an on-site deli and a from-scratch bakery, so you can take your goodies to go.

Another Italian favorite is **Giamano's** (301 Main St., 732/775-4275, www.giamanos.com, Tues.–Sun. from 5 P.M., closed Mon., $15–25), a classy restaurant with a downstairs dining room and outdoor café, and a second-floor live music lounge known for its jazz and blues. Traditional dishes include pasta marinara ($13.95) and shrimp scampi ($23.95).

Bradley Beach staple **Vic's** (60 Main St., 732/774-8225, www.vicspizza.com, Tues.–Thurs. 11:30 A.M.–11 P.M., Fri.–Sat. 11:30 A.M.–midnight, Sun. noon–11 P.M.,

closed Mon., year-round, $13–19) has been dishing up superb thin-crusted pizzas and pastas doused in homemade sauce since 1947. With its paneled walls and a number board that lights when order are up, the interior doesn't seem to have changed much over the years, but this hasn't stopped crowds from coming. The joint gets packed even early in the evening, but ample indoor and outdoor seating makes for quick turnover.

Getting There and Around

NJ Transit's **North Jersey Coast Line** from New York City stops in Bradley Beach. The borough is located east of the Garden State Parkway, Exit 100. After exiting, take Route 33 to Ocean Grove. Bradley Beach is the next town south.

BELMAR

With a lively nightlife and a full social calendar, not to mention a spectacular beach, Belmar is bustling. Long known as a retreat for rowdy grads and college parties, the borough is in the midst of an image makeover. Regulations on the number of renters to each summer unit and club noise restrictions are evidence of Belmar's shifting population. Still, while afternoon activities, including several weekend festivals and the state's largest St. Patty's Day parade, are popular borough pastimes, nightlife reigns supreme in Belmar and neighboring **Lake Como.** Downtown is filled with bars and restaurants, many of which are open year-round. With so much going on, it's little surprise legendary Captain Kidd is rumored to have buried treasure here (no doubt after a night at the pub).

Belmar is located between the Shark River and the Atlantic Ocean, with Silver Lake to the north of town and Lake Como to the south. It's home to New Jersey's largest commercial marina and a mile-long semicommercial boardwalk.

Beaches

Belmar's daily beach tags cost $7, age 14 and under free. A season pass costs $50. Alcohol is not permitted. Parking along the beach is mostly metered, but free spots can be had if you're willing to walk.

The borough hosts designated beaches for each of its water sports. Surfing is allowed south of the 16th Avenue jetty and on both sides of the 19th Avenue jetty. Kayaks are permitted south of 20th Avenue. For boogie boarders, the best ocean beaches are between 13th and 19th Avenues. Surf fishers should hit the Shark River inlet.

In addition to the ocean beaches there's a sandy artificial beach at L Street along the Shark River.

Events

Belmar and Lake Como play joint host to the state's largest **St. Patrick's Day Parade** (www .belmarparade.com), complete with bagpipers and marching bands, paving way for a daylong celebration that includes traditional Irish fare and green beer galore.

Belmar's long-running two-day **New Jersey Seafood Festival** (Silver Lake Park on Ocean Ave. between 5th and 6th Aves., 732/774-8506, www.belmar.com), held annually in June, features more than 45 seafood vendors with samples of everything from crab cakes to fresh steamed lobster. An international wine tent serves to complement local fare. Free festival trolley service runs between Belmar Marina, the NJ Transit train station, the beach, and the festival grounds.

Score prizes for the most creative or elaborate sand sculpture at the **New Jersey Sand Castle Contest** (732/681-3700, www.belmar .com), held on the beach in early July. Anyone can participate, but be warned: There are some true sand masters at work.

After two years in Seaside Heights, the three-day **AVP Volleyball Tournament** (732/681-3700, www.belmar.com, http://web.avp.com) returned to Belmar in June 2008, and many residents are hoping it's back to stay. Part of a cross-country tour, the tournament attracts thousands to Belmar's beaches to see some of the world's best pro volleyball players serve, block, pass, and dig.

Free family movies screen Sunday evenings throughout the summer at 8th Street beach, beginning at dusk. Visit www.belmar.com for a full schedule.

Sports and Recreation

The **Belmar Marina** (Rte. 35 and 10th Ave., 732/681-5005) is New Jersey's largest commercial marina. No wonder sportfishing is such a popular local activity—you've got dozens of charter boats and fishing party vessels to choose from. For deep-sea fishing try the 100-passenger **Suzie Girl** (732/988-7760), or for something smaller, the six-person sportfishing boat **Teri Jean II** (732/280-7364, www.terijean.com). For diving excursions call Dean Iglay at **Horizon** (732/280-3284). Bait and tackle shop **Fisherman's Den** (Rte. 35, 732/681-5005, www.fishermansdennj. com) rents motorboats for use on the Shark River ($59.95 per day). The river hosts flounder, fluke, and striped bass, as well as blue-claw crabs late in the summer season.

During summer months, bicycles are only permitted on the boardwalk before 8 A.M. and after 8 P.M.

Nightlife

Belmar is known for its nightlife, although it's not the all-night partying of Seaside or the nonstop gluttony Atlantic City can be. It's more of the drinking beer, snacking on wings, and chilling outdoors kind of nightlife, with some dancing (and shots) thrown in for good measure. The following spots are known for their nightlife, but all serve food during the day and early evening. Like most Belmar establishments they're open year-round.

Known as "Bar A" to insiders, Lake Como's **Bar Anticipation** (703-705 16th Ave., 732/681-7422, www.bar-a.com, daily 10 A.M.–2 A.M.) is open all year, but the party really picks up in summer, with beat-the-clock Tuesdays and original band night Wednesdays, Saturday night danceathons, and all-you-can-eat seafood Sundays. Revelers make the most of the outdoor deck, downing $2 drafts and munching on pizza, burgers, and spicy Cajun tidbits. Did I mention drink specials?

With more than 30 satellite HD TVs, a

pool-table room, 14 beers on tap, and a waterproof smoking area, the **Boathouse Bar & Grill** (1309 Main St., 732/681-5221, www.boathousebarandgrill.com, Mon.–Sat. 11 A.M.–2 A.M., Sun. noon–2 A.M.) has got to be the best sports bar in town. A seven-days-a-week Irish happy hour doesn't hurt matters, nor do specials like beach badge giveaways. Wireless Internet too? You could live here.

I'm guessing you're coming for the drinks, but **Patrick's Pub** (711 Main St., 732/280-2266) is also rumored to cook some of the best steaks at the Jersey Shore. This tavern features live bands weekly, along with a fine wraparound bar.

Accommodations

Belmar's overnight choices include hotels, B&Bs, and a couple of guesthouses, though the borough's inability to shake its party reputation keeps many places average at best. These are the borough's standouts, and both offer complimentary breakfast daily.

An easy walk from the beach is the **Morning Dove B&B** (204 5th Ave., 732/556-0777, www.morningdoveinn.com, $175–270), a converted 19th-century Victorian home with eight guest rooms—including two suites—and a solarium overlooking Silver Lake. All rooms have air-conditioning and private baths, and guests are allowed access to the inn's private garden.

Also bordering Silver Lake is **The Inn at the Shore** (301 4th Ave., 732/681-3762, www.theinnattheshore.com, $175–285), a family-friendly B&B with 11 uniquely styled guest rooms. This 19th-century Victorian features a wraparound porch dotted with gliders and rocking chairs, a freshwater aquarium (for the kids), and a quiet reading and writing area. Though decor goes the way of ruffled curtains and teddy bears, at least it's not gloomy. Some rooms have shared baths.

Food

It's easy to find something to snack on along Belmar's boardwalk, but for more of a restaurant feel head inland to downtown and along the Shark River.

For coffee and doughnuts stop by downtown's **Freedman's Bakery** (803 Main St., 732/681-2334)—you can't miss its retro sign. Take a seat at the counter or box the sweet stuff to go. Breakfast and lunch is served beginning at 6 A.M.

One of only several vegetarian restaurants in New Jersey, **Kaya's Kitchen** (817 Belmar Plaza, 732/280-1141, www.kayaskitchennj.com, $8–16) has quite a loyal following. Some dishes—like a "sloppy joe" sandwich smothered in barbecue sauce ($10), and country fried soy legs ($14.95)—are vegan-friendly and have even been known to convert meat eaters. Nachos ($9) and soy nuggets ($6) are especially good appetizers. Kaya's menu is both eclectic and extensive and includes a seasonal Sunday breakfast; BYO. Lunch hours are Tuesday–Saturday 11:30 A.M.–2:30 P.M., and dinner is Tuesday–Saturday 5 P.M.–10 P.M. Breakfast is served seasonally (Apr.–Oct.) Sunday 9 A.M.–1 P.M. Sunday night features an all-you-can-eat vegan buffet, 5 P.M.–9 P.M. Closed Monday.

Dining at **Brandl** (703 Belmar Plaza, 732/280-7501, www.brandlrestaurant.com, dinner Mon.–Thurs. 5–10 P.M., Fri.–Sat. 5–11 P.M., Sun. 5–9 P.M., year-round, $24–38) is more like being in the big city than at the Jersey Shore. Though its storefront exterior gives little indication, Brandl is completely cosmopolitan—in decor, taste, and price. A seasonally refined New American menu most always features chef Chris Brandl's signature crab cakes ($14), which guests can savor on the heated outdoor patio. Friday nights are reserved for live jazz; additional entertainment has included Sinatra nights and psychic readings.

One of Belmar's most beloved institutions is **Klein's Fish Market and Waterside Cafe** (708 River Rd., 732/681-1177, www.kleinsfishmarketonline.com, Sun.–Thurs. 11:30 A.M.–9 P.M., Fri.–Sat. 11:30 A.M.–10 P.M., brunch Sun. 11 A.M.–3 P.M., year-round, $11–22), in business since 1929. Grab an indoor table or a dockside seat outdoors overlooking the Shark River—either way the fresh no-nonsense seafood is fantastic. T-shirts and flip-flops are standard attire, and a sushi bar adds a touch of the exotic. Sunday brunch ($18.95 adult, $5.95 child) also receives top ratings.

Matisse (13th and Ocean Aves., 732/681-7680, www.matissecatering.com, $24–36) offers seasonal fine dining with unbeatable oceanfront views. This Grecian-style BYO restaurant is a bit more refined than your typical boardwalk eatery. Dishes include sweet and spicy Szechwan shrimp and Canadian hard-shelled lobster. During fall and winter Matisse hosts a Sunday interactive brunch, inviting guests to enter the kitchen and choose from five hot entrées, which the chef then prepares. Summer hours are nightly 5:30–10 P.M. July–August, closed Tuesdays in June.

Getting There

Belmar is located off Exit 98 of the Garden State Parkway. Its train station is located at downtown's Belmar Plaza between Ninth and 10th Avenues, within easy walking distance of restaurants. To reach Belmar from New York City and the Gateway Region by train, take NJ Transit's North Jersey Coast Line.

◖ SPRING LAKE

A throwback to yesteryear, elegant Spring Lake remains one of the last authenticities of the grand ol' Jersey Shore. Both picturesque and peaceful, this affluent borough is brimming with Victorian homes, stately beachfront hotels, and bed-and-breakfasts that line the streets and surround the namesake lake. Downtown's Third Avenue hosts some of the Shore's best shopping, and a few of the North Shore's best restaurants are found here as well. Unlike most shore towns, Spring Lake is primarily a year-round residential community. Most visitors stay at one of the more than dozen recommendable accommodation options throughout town. The beachfront features a two-mile noncommercial boardwalk (the state's longest noncommercial boardwalk) made from recycled plastic and perfect for savoring ocean views.

Beaches

Spring Lake's daily beach tags cost $8, age 12

and under free. Tags are also available for a half season ($60) or full season ($100). During summer months no food or drink is permitted on the beach, but *New Jersey Monthly* suggests leaving a snack-filled cooler along the two-mile boardwalk until you're ready to chow down.

Events

The **Spring Lake Chamber of Commerce** (304 Washington Ave., 732/449-0577, www.springlake.org) sponsors an annual **Bed & Breakfast Christmas Candlelight Tour** in early December, along with various summer happenings. Visit their website for a complete schedule. The borough's **Community House Theatre** (3rd and Madison Ave., 732/449-4530, springlaketheatre.com, $26 adult, $20 child) hosts locally produced musicals and plays throughout the year. Recently performances include *The Producers* and *Gaslight,* a psychological thriller.

Shopping

The borough's shopping district is centered along downtown's Third Avenue. Although it's a bit of a walk from the beach, it's a pleasant one, and once here you'll find plenty of specialty shops, boutiques, galleries, and candy counters to keep you occupied. Downtown shops remain open until 8 P.M. the fourth Friday of every month throughout summer.

BOUTIQUES AND SPECIALTY SHOPS

Camel's Eye (1223 3rd Ave., 732/449-3636) stocks funky designer fashions and Crocs wide-toed shoes, bright bags by Hobo and Kipling, and an assortment of distinguishing hairclips. The tiny **Teddy Bears by the Seashore** (1306 3rd Ave., 732/449-7446) is packed with Jersey-centric hats, sweats, and T-shirts for adults and kids, in addition to Jersey Girl dolls and a teddy bear collection. Girls are queen bee at **Splash** (1305 3rd Ave., 732/449-8388), a favorite clothing boutique of hip moms and daughters.

Men who prefer plaid shorts, Venetian leather shoes, and alpaca sweaters should hit **Village Tweed** (1213 3rd Ave., 732/449-2723, www.villagetweedinc.com), a Spring Lake institution since 1977. For surf and skate fashionistas there's **Third Avenue Surf Shop** (1206 3rd Ave., 732/449-1866, www.3rdavesurf.com), carrying clothing and gear from designers like Oakley, O'Neill, and Smith.

Home and body boutique **Urban Details** (1111 3rd Ave., 732/282-0013, www.urban-details.com) sells handblown glass and jewelry, along with wind chimes, clean-burning candles, and milk shampoo.

GALLERIES AND ANTIQUES

Located just north of the main shopping strip, **Thistledown Gallery Framing** (1045 3rd Ave., 732/974-0376) showcases fine art, including acrylics, watercolors, and lithographs, of local and national artists. The gallery specializes in framing and offers limited-edition prints for purchase.

Evergreen Gallery (308 Morris Ave., 732/449-4488) displays and sells a wonderful array of photography, fine art, and mixed-media works created by New Jersey artists.

Allison's Attic (1317 3rd Ave., 732/449-3485) carries a fun selection of 20th-century antiques, including a Mickey Mantle–signed blueprint of Yankee Stadium and a framed dinner menu from Spring Lake's former Monmouth Hotel.

CANDY STORES

Chocolate comes in all shapes and sizes at **Jean Louise Homemade Candies** (1025 3rd Ave., 732/449-2627), a Spring Lake landmark for more than 85 years. While the chocolate-covered strawberries are to die for, you also have chocolate-shaped baseball gloves, seashells, and elves to choose from. For saltwater taffy and chocolate pops shaped like cartoon characters, try **Third Avenue Chocolate Shoppe** (1138 3rd Ave., 732/449-7535) across the street. Their "chicken legs" on a stick are a must!

Accommodations

Historic hotels, inns, and B&Bs are both plentiful and worth the splurge in this upscale resort. Approximately a dozen of them are registered with the **Historic Inns of Spring Lake** (732/859-1465, www.historicinnsof springlake.com), which hosts events that include the award-winning **Authors and Inns Tour** each June.

The **White Lilac Inn** (414 Central Ave., 732/449-0211, www.whitelilac.com, $179–359) features nine guest rooms ranging from the woodsy Vermont cabin room to the Studio, doused in the rich red hue of a box of Valentines chocolates. Rooms include cable TV and air-conditioning, and some come with old-fashion soaking tubs.

Close to Spring Lake's train station and downtown shopping district is the **Chateau Inn and Suites** (500 Warren Ave, 732/974-2000, www.chateauinn.com). Housed in a late-19th-century building, the 37-room boutique hotel has been updated with modern amenities, including high-speed Internet, plasma TVs, and marble bathtubs. Some rooms have patios, fireplaces, and French doors. In addition to overnight rates, the inn offers celebratory packages such as spa trips and romance-themed room service.

The elegant **Normandy Inn** (21 Tuttle Ave., 732/449-7172, www.normandyinn.com, $149–399) is a late-19th-century Italianate villa listed on the National Register of Historic Places. With 16 rooms and two suites, all decorated in a classic Victorian motif, this is one of the borough's larger B&Bs. Despite its throwback decor, all rooms feature private baths, TVs, high-speed Internet, and air-conditioning, and some have Jacuzzis and fireplaces. A gourmet breakfast prepared by chefs from the French Culinary Institute (no, you're not dreaming) is served to guests restaurant-style.

Spread on prime oceanfront property is the historic 73-room **Breakers Hotel** (1507 Ocean Ave., 732/449-7700, www.breakershotel.com, $220–435), an imposing white clapboard more than a century old. The hotel's beach is private, although there's also an in-ground pool with dining nearby. Size and location make the Breakers a popular place for wedding receptions and conferences, and noise can sometimes be a problem—requesting a room away from the banquet hall may help. All rooms come with high-speed Internet access and a fridge, and many offer incredible ocean views.

Only a block from the beach is **Ashling Cottage B&B** (106 Sussex Ave., 732/449-3553, www.ashlingcottage.com, closed Jan.–Feb., $215–295), a 19th-century Victorian with 11 uniquely designed guest rooms and a glass atrium where visitors can linger over morning meals. The rooms, fairly bright and simple in decor, are spread over three floors (those on the bottom floors are largest). Guests are allowed use of the inn's bicycles during their stay, and there's also a hammock for snoozing, and a covered front porch perfect for an afternoon reprieve.

Housed in an 1888 shingled Victorian originally built as the borough's Grand Central Stables, the 🄲 **Spring Lake Inn** (104 Salem Ave., 732/449-2010 or 800/803-9031, www.springlakeinn.com, $219–399) is a find. There are 16 guest rooms, each painted in rich hues that complement their themes. Personal touches include a telescope in the Moonbeam Room, a sleigh bed in the Tower View, and the Lighthouse Room's maritime decor. Guests can spend the afternoon rocking in chairs on the inn's 80-foot covered porch, taking advantage of complimentary beach tags and towels, or using the inn's gym passes. The borough's beach and boardwalk are only a block away. Most rooms come equipped with a private bath, and all feature full breakfast daily.

Food

Spring Lake hosts a couple of upscale restaurants, along with more casual eateries along its downtown Third Avenue strip.

The Gulf Coast–inspired BYO **Island Palm Grill** (1321 3rd Ave., 732/449-1909, www.islandpalmgrill.com, Tues.–Sat. 11 A.M.–3 P.M. and 5:30–9 P.M., Sun. 10 A.M.–2 P.M. and 5:30–9 P.M. summer) features an ever-changing menu of dishes like lobster ravioli in lump-crab brandy sauce ($25) and plantain-crusted grouper ($24). A gracious staff helps with your selections.

Tucked within the lakefront Hewitt-Wellington Hotel (www.hewittwellington.com), BYO **Whispers** (200 Monmouth Ave., 732/974-9755, www.whispersrestaurant.com, daily 5:30 P.M.–midnight, $29–34) provides a feast of culinary offerings in a lavish elegant setting. Globally inspired dishes range from a relatively simple grilled salmon filet with mango salsa ($29) to a double-cut pork chop topped with Applewood bacon barbecue sauce ($29).

Situated on the ground floor of the historic Sandpiper Inn is the trendy **Black Trumpet** (7 Atlantic Ave., 732/449-4700, www.theblacktrumpet.com, lunch daily 11:30 A.M.–2 P.M. summer beginning in May, dinner Mon.–Thurs. 5–9 P.M., Fri.–Sat. 5–10 P.M., Sun. 4–8 P.M., $20–31), a BYO serving up New American cuisine with a creative flair. Chefs Mark Mikolajczyk and Dave McCleery are both alums of nearby Whispers, and seafood is their specialty. Of course desserts are just as fabulous, and are prepared either at your table or fresh in the kitchen daily. If you need further incentive to take on extra calories, remember, you can always walk along the beach afterward: It's literally right out the door.

Families flock to **Who's on Third?** (1300 3rd Ave., 732/449-4233, $5–21), a downtown deli and grill serving breakfast and lunch, as well as dinner in-season. Score a stool at the lunch counter and sit back with a pork roll sandwich while admiring framed images of baseball's greats.

Getting There

Spring Lake is located off Exit 98 of the Garden State Parkway. The borough's train station, accessible from New York City by NJ Transit's North Shore Line, is within walking distance of downtown's Third Avenue. The ride is approximately two hours from start to finish.

SEA GIRT AND MANASQUAN

Just south of Spring Lake is Sea Girt, an affluent community filled with sizable homes, manicured lawns, and an unusually high number of parked Mercedes. Although it doesn't offer much of a Shore feel, that's easy to find in nearby Manasquan, a cozy borough replete with funky beach shacks and bungalows, and more of a jeep-driving crowd. Long boards, beach cruisers, and hippie teens are in great supply here, giving Manasquan a sort of Santa Cruz, California, feel. The borough has both ocean and inlet beaches, and hosts some of the best surfing in the state.

Sea Girt Lighthouse

Built in 1896 to bridge a 40-mile gap between the Twin Lights of Navesink and Long Beach Island's Old Barney, the nonoperational Sea Girt Lighthouse (Ocean and Baltimore Blvd.) was the last live-in lighthouse constructed along the country's Atlantic Coast. The structure itself—an inconspicuous though pretty brick Victorian across the street from the beach—is easily overlooked, but once you find it, historic maps, photos, and lighthouse memorabilia make the inside worth a peek. Tours are conducted Sundays through mid-November (2–4 P.M.) and include the lighthouse keeper's office, the Fresnel lens room, and the tower. For further details, call the lighthouse message line at 732/974-0514.

Beaches

Sea Girt's daily beach tags cost $7 adult, age 12 and under free, and a season pass costs $70. For Manasquan, daily beach tags cost $6 adult weekdays and $7 weekends, age 12 and under free; a season pass costs $60.

One of the best surfing spots along the entire Jersey Shore is Manasquan's **Inlet Beach,** also a favorite fishing locale and one of the state's most easily accessible beaches. There's ample handicap parking nearby and a wooden walk that crosses the sand to a viewing area, ideal for mobility-impaired people.

Accommodations

Opened in 2004, Manasquan's **Inn on Main** (152 Main St., 732/528-0809, www.innon mainmanasquan.com, $199–269) stands along the town's small bustling Main Street. This boutique hotel features 12 individually styled rooms, each with its own personality.

Room 301 gets the morning sun, while rooms 204 and 304 are perfect for those traveling with kids. The country decor of room 201 is a grandparent favorite.

Food

Between Sea Girt and Manasquan you'll have plenty of restaurants to choose from. Most casual spots are located along Manasquan's waterfront, while more upscale eateries are scattered throughout Sea Girt and Manasquan's downtown Main Street, some distance from the ocean beach.

Sea Girt's seasonal ◖ **Parker House** (1st and Beacon Ave., Sea Girt, 732/449-0442, www.parkerhousenj.com, $10–27) is an area institution, a glorious old clapboard Victorian strung with white lights during summer months, offering live music, dancing, and tavern-style dishes served outdoors on its wrap-around veranda. The converted home was built in 1878 and continues to house apartment units up top. In addition to pub food there's an upscale steak and seafood restaurant on the structure's main floor, right above a tavern and below a nightclub. During the day the Parker House attracts families and beachgoers, but nights are taken over by a 20- and 30-something crowd; a group, I might add, that likes to drink.

Just south of Sea Girt on the drive into Manasquan is **Surf Taco** (121 Parker Ave., 732/223-7757, www.surftaco.com, Sun.–Thurs. 11 A.M.–9 P.M., Fri.–Sat. 11 A.M.–9:30 P.M., $2.95–9.95), a Shore semi-chain serving Cal-Mex eats in a brightly painted surf shack. Order at the counter, then grab a table in back among the local teen crowd.

Across the street from the beach where Manasquan's inlet and ocean meet, the flip-flop casual **Riverside Café** (425 Riverside Dr., 732/223-2233, $7–12) offers indoor and outdoor seating, along with burgers, grilled sandwiches, and some of the best chocolate shakes around.

Gracing downtown's Main Street is stylish **Mahogany Grille** (142 Main St., 732/292-1300, www.themahoganygrille.com, Mon.–Thurs.

5–10 P.M., Fri.–Sat. 5–11 P.M., Sun. 4–9 P.M., $24–36), a white-linen restaurant serving some of the Shore's best cuisine. Entrées include filet medallions in red wine syrup ($32) and peppercorn-crusted tuna with sweet brown rice ($30). Proper dress is required. Call for off-season hours.

Local hangout **Green Planet Coffee** (78 Main St., Manasquan 732/722-8197) serves organic and fair-trade coffee along with a small selection of pastries. Local artwork hangs on the walls, but you may be too busy connecting to the free Wi-Fi to notice.

Getting There
NJ Transit's **North Jersey Coast Line** stops at Manasquan's train station, just east of Main Street. To reach Manasquan by car, take Route 35 to the Manasquan Circle, following Atlantic Avenue East until it ends. Make a right onto Broad Street and follow it to the end. Turn left onto Main Street.

The Barnegat Peninsula

Referred to as Barnegat Peninsula from its days before the Point Pleasant Canal was added, this stretch of land starts north at Point Pleasant and continues to the southern tip of Island Beach State Park. North and Central Jersey's best boardwalks are found here, along with one of the most pristine and extensive white-sand beaches along the entire Jersey coast.

POINT PLEASANT BEACH
Not to be mistaken for the nearby borough sharing its name, family-friendly Point Pleasant Beach began as a fishing village that gained popularity once the railroad came to town, and only increased in appeal when the Garden State Parkway opened. Grassy-lawn Cape Cods and bungalows are the typical town residences. Downtown hovers around Arnold, Bay, and Richmond Streets, where there are several restaurants and bars and at least one coffeehouse. Still, the boardwalk is the town's main attraction, especially for kids and teens.

Sights
It may not be the Shore's longest walkway, but **Jenkinson's Boardwalk** (300 Ocean Ave., 732/892-0600, www.jenkinsons.com) packs a lot in for its size. Its two ends are mostly non-commercial, perfect for joggers and casual strollers. For action, head toward the center—a conglomeration of custard stands, pizza places, carnival games, and casual bars built up on both sides in seaworthy shades of green, blue, and pink. Jenkinson's hosts an aquarium and an outdoor amusement park geared towards kids (www.jenkinsons.com, opens daily at noon during summer), but perhaps its best attraction is the **Fun House** ($5), two stories of trick mirrors, moving floors, air blasts, and a rotating tunnel—the kind John Travolta and Olivia Newton John dance on at the end of *Grease.*

Open year-round, privately owned **Jenkinson's Aquarium** (300 Ocean Ave., 732/899-1212, www.jenkinsons.com, Mon.–Fri. 9:30 A.M.–5 P.M., Sat.–Sun. 10 A.M.–5 P.M., $10 adult, $6 senior and child) is a class-trip favorite. First-floor exhibits include tropical fish, sharks, gators, and underwater penguins, while the second floor features a rainforest exhibit with macaws, hissing cockroaches, poison dart frogs, and pygmy marmosets—the world's smallest monkeys. Scheduled shark feedings are open to the public throughout the year.

Beaches
Daily beach tags cost $6.50 on weekdays, $7.50 adult, $2 ages 5–11 on weekends. An adult season pass costs $80, and $45 ages 5–11. Point Pleasant's beaches are both public and private access. There's a small fee to access public beaches along the south end of town. To use the beaches in front of the boardwalk, tags must be purchased directly from Jenkinson's. Stations exist at most entryways.

Fun House, Jenkinson's Boardwalk

Surfers gather off-hours at the Pocket along Point Pleasant's inlet to catch waves, but surfing-permitted beaches are difficult to find during on-hours. Your best bet is to drive down to Manasquan. Alcohol is not permitted on Jenkinson's Beach (except in front of the Tiki Bar), but coolers are allowed.

Entertainment and Events
The Southern-style *River Belle* (732/892-3377, www.riverboattour.com) riverboat leaves on two-hour sightseeing tours ($17 adult, $8.25 child) along Barnegat Bay and Point Pleasant Canal daily except Sunday during July and August. Advance tickets are recommended. Additional cruises, such as a Pizza and Fireworks Cruise ($33 adult, $22 child) and a Murder Mystery Dinner Cruise ($62), are scheduled throughout summer. The *River Belle* is docked along the Point Pleasant Canal, leaving from Broadway Basin (47 Broadway Pt.).

Ditch your winter parka, don your skimpiest suit, and join dozens of other maniacs in February's annual **Polar Bear Plunge** (732/213-5387), an ocean dip raising money for the Special Olympics.

Movies on the Beach (732/892-0600) are screened on scheduled summer evenings at Jenkinson's beach in front of the boardwalk. Past flicks have included *National Treasure: Book of Secrets* and *Enchanted*.

Since 1975, September's **Festival of the Sea** (www.pointpleasantbeach.com/seafood festival.htm) has signaled summer's end with a showcase of arts and crafts and antiques, local foods, and loads of entertainment. Free shuttles run from the boardwalk to downtown festival grounds.

Sports and Recreation
The charter boat *Diversion II* (http://njscuba .net) takes pro divers to explore artificial reefs and real shipwrecks off New Jersey's coast. For more information contact Captain Steve Nagiewicz by email at steve@njscuba.com.

The **New Jersey Sailing School** (1800 Bay Ave., 732/295-3450, www.newjersey sailingschool.com) offers multiday lessons in basic sailing ($319), bareboat chartering ($579), and coastal navigation ($249). Most workshops are held during summer months, but a few are available in the off-season. Check the website for a complete schedule.

The inlet between Point Pleasant Beach and Manasquan, also known as "The Wall," is one of the area's best fishing spots, and a good place for charter boat rentals. Two to try are **Gambler Fishing** (59 Inlet Dr., 732/295-7569, www.gamblerfishing.net), with twice-daily fluke-fishing trips and night bluefish trips illuminated by underwater lights, and **Purple Jet Sportfishing Fleet** (Canyon River Club, 407 Channel Dr., 732/996-2579 or 800/780-8862, www.purplejet.com), running six-person Atlantic Ocean charter trips. Need fishing supplies? Stop by **Alex's Bait and Tackle** (9 Inlet Dr., 732/295-9268, www.baitandtackle .tv). Public restrooms are located on the inlet's eastern side.

Daredevils may want to try **Point Pleasant Parasail** (Ken's Landing, 30 Broadway,

732/714-2359, www.pointpleasantparasail
.org). Solo flights 500 feet above the sea cost
$65; if you'd rather go side-by-side with a
friend, it's $120. Ocean "dips" are offered for
the more adventurous.

Accommodations

Although it's nothing fancy, Point Pleasant
Beach's **Windswept Motel** (1008 Beach Ave.,
732/899-1282, windsweptmotel.net, $168–258
s, $203–293 d) gets high marks for cleanli-
ness and value. It's within walking distance of
both the beach and the boardwalk, and there's
a small pool on-site. Some rooms even have
ocean views.

Close to Point Pleasant inlet is the family-owned **Surfside Motel** (101 Broadway,
732/899-1109, www.surfside-motel.com, $160–
280). Clean standard rooms come equipped
with a TV and a fridge, air-conditioning, and
complimentary use of daily beach tags. There's
also a heated in-ground pool roadside.

The upscale **White Sands Oceanfront
Resort & Spa** (1205 Ocean Ave., 732/899-
3370, www.thewhitesands.com, $260–765)
features both a beachfront motel and a fancier
hotel across the street. With two outdoor pools
and a private beach, the 74-room motel is the
more family-friendly of the two, while a highlight of the 56-room hotel is an adults-only
spa. Shared amenities include an Italian steakhouse, fitness club, martini and frozen-drink
bar, and an on-site liquor store.

Food and Nightlife

For a hot dog and cold beer, stop by
Jenkinson's Inlet Restaurant (1 Point
Pleasant Beach, 732/892-0234) on the north
end of the boardwalk. Its decorative surf-
boards and open-air bar give off sort of an island feel—and with the ocean stretched before
you, it'll be closing time before you known it.
Central to the boards is **Jenkinson's Pavilion**
(300 Boardwalk, 732/899-0569) a large space
hosting several bars and eateries, including a
full-service American restaurant, a sushi bar,
and an always-packed fast-food counter serving exceptional pepperoni pizza slices ($4).

Tucked away in the rear is **Martell's Tiki Bar**
(312 Boardwalk, 732/892-0131, www.tikibar.
com, call for hours), *the* place for frozen margaritas and daiquiris. Enjoy them ocean-side
along the pier or beach on sticky summer evenings while live bands perform. The pavilion
opens daily at 11 A.M. during summer. Tiki
bar hours vary so call ahead, or check out the
website's webcam to see what's happening in
real time.

For gourmet pizza try local favorite **Joey
Tomatoes** (Central Ave. and Boardwalk,
732/295-2624, daily in summer, $3–15). Order
a slice of chicken parm and linger at one of
the boardwalk tables while enjoying supreme
people-watching.

Since the 1950s, ◖ **Co-op Seafood &
Market** (57 Channel Dr., 732/899-2211, daily
10 A.M.–9 P.M. summer, daily 10 A.M.–6 P.M.
off-season, $8.50–15) has been serving fresh
fish straight from the boats of the local fishers who own it. Just a handful of tables line
the inside windows of this small no-frills

sign for the kitschy Circus Drive-In along
Route 35

establishment, but there's plenty of picnic seating out front. Portions are large, and the staff is both knowledgeable and friendly.

A bit north of Point Pleasant Beach along Route 35 is the glorious **Circus Drive-In** (1861 State Rte. 35, 732/449-2650, www.circus drivein.com, daily 11 A.M.–9 P.M.), a must-stop for fans of roadside architecture and fat pork-roll clubs ($5.99). The 1954 Circus is one of New Jersey's (and the country's) last remaining carhop eateries, and it's in tip-top shape. Pull in for a malted shake and a Wild Animal (ground beef) special ($6.39)—a smiling-clown sign and a circus tent awning leads the way.

Getting There

Point Pleasant Beach is located off Exit 98 (southbound) or Exit 90 (northbound) of the Garden State Parkway. NJ Transit's **North Jersey Coast Line** arrives from New York City at Point Pleasant's downtown train station at Arnold Avenue and Route 35. The station is only a few feet away from downtown's shops and eateries and a few blocks from the beach and boardwalk.

BAY HEAD

It's easy to understand where Bay Head got its nickname, "The New England of the Jersey Shore": With its weathered wood-shingled homes and a charming main street, this hamlet feels like an ideal fit for Martha's Vineyard. Barnegat Bay passes beneath downtown's tiny Bridge Avenue, home to a handful of specialty shops and a sweet bakery, and just north along Lake Avenue, bayside benches offer reprieve among ducks and various shorebirds. For anyone needing a vacation from their vacation, this is the place to come.

Beaches

Daily beach tags cost $6 adult, age 12 and under free. An adult season pass cost $65 or $45 for a half-season. Parking throughout town is free. Due to its small size and lack of tourist attractions, Bay Head offers no public restrooms or changing rooms. Food and beverages are prohibited on the beach.

Shopping

Most Bay Head shops are centered along Bridge Avenue, with a handful of stores scattered throughout town.

Old-fashioned **Mueller's Bakery** (80 Bridge Ave., 732/892-0442, www.muellers bakery.com) smells of baked butter cookies and cheese-filled pastries. Lines can be long, so get here early.

For beach-blanket and tote-bag combos, handmade Jersey Girl plaques, and a variety of antiques and collectibles, check out **Cobwebs** (64 Bridge Ave., 732/892-8005). Both a gift shop and art gallery, **The Jolly Tar** (56 Bridge Ave., 732/892-0223) carries specialty writing paper and hand-carved decoys, and keeps a full-time bridal consultant on staff.

Walking through the **Shopper's Wharf** (70 Bridge Ave., 732/295-4333), a former historic theater, is like entering a cartoon village: Store exteriors are painted to look like they're outdoors. Selections in this makeshift miniature town include the tiny tea and coffee shop **Bay Head Blends,** beach-themed jewelry store **Memory Shoppe,** and the **Chocolate Shoppe** (732/899-2870), selling homemade chocolates and fudge for more than 30 years.

Accommodations

The Queen Anne–style **Bentley Inn** (694 Main Ave., 732/892-9589 or 866/423-6853, www.bentleyinn.com, $164–249 s, $194–279 d) features 19 brightly colored guest rooms, most with a shared bath and all with a TV and VCR, air-conditioning, and individual sitting areas. The inn is known for its expansive covered porches and a dining solarium where guests dine on Belgium waffles and caramelized French toast. Use of the inn's bikes is complimentary.

Conover's Bay Head Inn (646 Main Ave., 732/892-8748, www.conovers.com, $175–320) hosts nine antique-filled guest rooms and three suites, all with a private bath, TV and VCR, and air-conditioning. Fresh baked goods are offered daily to enjoy outdoors in the inn's English garden or with afternoon tea.

Food

Nestled below Bay Head's **Historic Grenville Hotel** (345 Main Ave., 732/892-3100, www.thegrenville.com, Mon.–Fri. 11:30 A.M.–2:30 P.M. and 5–9 P.M., Sat. 11:30 A.M.–2:30 P.M. and 5–9:30 P.M., Sun. 9:30 A.M.–1:30 P.M. and 5–9 P.M., $18–40), the Grenville restaurant is this hamlet's fine-dining gem, a place to celebrate anniversaries and promotions. New American dishes come served in a Victorian setting or along an expansive front porch. The Sunday brunch buffet is a highlight.

Getting There

Bay Head is located off Exit 98 (southbound) or Exit 90 (northbound) of the Garden State Parkway. New Jersey Transit's **North Jersey Coast Line** runs from New York City to Bay Head, this small seaside hamlet being the last stop on the line.

SEASIDE HEIGHTS

It has been over a decade since Seaside Heights played host to MTV's summer beach house. If this gives any indication of what the town was like, things haven't changed. Dance clubs pumping pulsating music till the early morning, seedy motels advertising prom-night specials, and a tacky boardwalk topped with Muffler Men (those multistory fiberglass giants sometimes seen standing along secondary highways), Jäger bars, and casino arcades pretty much sum it up. For anyone wanting to partake in the Seaside spirit, stop by a boardwalk shop and buy yourself a "what happens in seaside stays in seaside" T-shirt, or one that reads "not only am i cute, but i'm italian, too." Then primp for the numerous security cameras and hit the piers for one long carnival ride. You'll have a story to tell.

Unless this is your designated shore town (which is kind of like a middle name for New Jerseyans), the boardwalk and amusement piers are the only real reasons to visit Seaside, along with a few interesting bars and clubs. Dining and accommodations are not Seaside's highlights, although a couple of bars offer a decent food selection and you can always grab a snack on the boardwalk. There are a few motels in town that are by no means luxurious, but are OK should you decide to stay. If you don't mind driving, it's worth it to book a room in Bay Head or Point Pleasant to the north and visit Seaside for the day.

Boardwalk

People are strange, you say? You haven't seen anything until you've visited Seaside Height's boardwalk. A wilder version of the Cape's Wildwood, this boardwalk attracts the ballsy, busty, and beefy, who are happy to display their wares. Built up on both sides with amusement piers, arcades, fried-food stands, bars, carnival games, and T-shirt shacks, it's definitely a sight to see. Why not take it all in from above? A mile-long skyway extends along the walkway's beach side, advertising cool breezes from its open-air seats.

Goth teens tend to congregate where the boardwalk narrows, connecting with the recycled plastic planks of Seaside Park's beachfront.

On the boardwalk's south side is the ocean-facing **Casino Pier** (800 Ocean Terr., 732/793-6495, www.casinopiernj.com), home to a log flume, pirate's cavern, glass house, and one of the boardwalk's best attractions, the Gothic-style **Stillwalk Manor** dark ride. The pier also hosts **Rooftop Wacky Golf,** an 18-hole miniature golf course presided over by the Happy Half-wit Muffler Man. Casino Pier is open every day in July and August and through most of June, and weekends during the shoulder seasons beginning mid-March and ending mid-September. Each ride costs a varying number of tickets (3–10), available for purchase on-site.

Was Pac-Man fever driving you crazy during the '80s? Then consider Casino Arcade's **Flashback Arcade,** tucked behind the carousel house, a must-stop. Centipede, Ms. Pac-Man, Track and Field, Pole Position—they're all here, and keeping with the yesteryear theme, most games play for $0.25. Ventilation is a problem, but most players are too overcome with joy to notice.

Casino Pier's carousel house is home to one

of only two American carved antique carousels remaining in New Jersey. The **Floyd Moreland Carousel** (732/793-6489, www.magical carousel.com, $2) features over 2,000 bulbs, nearly 20 paintings, and a Wurlitzer Band organ with 105 wooden pipes.

At Casino Pier's recently renovated **Jenkinson's Breakwater Beach** (800 Ocean Terr., 732/793-6488, www.casinopiernj.com, $22.95 adult, $18.95 child 3-hour admission) waterslides wiggle, plunge, shoot, and loop. Less-adventurous types take to the hot-springs pools and lazy river, or sit steady at one of the new private cabanas ($60 for 3 hours). There's also a good-sized kids' play area.

With over 40 rides, including bumper cars, a loop roller coaster, and the 225-foot freefalling Tower of Fear, **Funtown Pier** (1930 Boardwalk, 732/830-7437, www.funtownpier.com, $25 for 45 ride tickets) lives up to its name. A lot of the rides are for kids, but the giant Ferris wheel and go-karts belong to anyone. The pier is open throughout summer.

Beaches

Daily beach tags cost $5 adult, age 12 and under free. The beach is free for everyone Wednesdays and Thursdays. Seaside's adult season beach passes are a steal at only $35. There's metered parking on the streets; spaces in lots cost $5–10.

In nearby Seaside Park, just south, a day at the beach is $8 adult, age 11 and under free.

Events

Casino Pier hosts free summer fireworks every Wednesday beginning at 9 P.M.

In need of a laugh? Check out September's annual **Clownfest** convention (www.clown fest.com). Although the five-day event consists mostly of classes and competitions, the boardwalk parade, held on the final Sunday, is open to all. Painted participants are easily spotted throughout town, until packing 12-deep into their buggies for the drive home.

Accommodations

Motels are Seaside's primary overnight options,

and while there are plenty of them, a large percentage are uninhabitable. Following are a few of your best options for staying in Seaside, although Bay Head and Point Pleasant Beach both offer a greater selection and are only a short drive away—so you can skip the endless party for a good night's sleep.

Yes, the walls are wood-paneled, but rooms at the **Colony Motel** (65 Hiering Ave., 732/830-2113, www.seasidecolonymotel.com, $99–149) are clean and spacious. This lodging was recently selected by *The Washington Post* as the place to stay in Seaside. Amenities include air-conditioning, fridges, microwaves, and an in-ground pool.

In a commendable effort to keep noise to a minimum, the 23-room **Luna Mar Motel** (1201 N. Ocean Ave., 732/793-8991 or 877/586-2627, www.lunamarmotel.com, $148–198) strictly enforces the policy that anyone age 21 and under must be accompanied by an adult. Focusing on families and couples, the motel offers quiet rooms and efficiencies, most with newly renovated baths and furnishings. There's a swimming pool on-site.

Food and Nightlife

For a taste of New Jersey the way the rest of the world imagines it (gold chains, fringe T-shirts, big hair, accents), there's no place better than Seaside. This doesn't mean every Seaside establishment is Jersified—there are a few local bars where the state stereotype is a minority. These are usually the best places to grab a bite to eat as well. Like other New Jersey shore towns, many Seaside Heights establishments taper business hours beginning in the fall until January, when they're locked and bolted until spring.

For Seaside Heights in all its glory, swing by **Merge** (302 Boulevard, 732/793-3111), a downtown dance club featuring its own private champagne bar. When resident DJ Richie Rydell spins underground club tunes, rumor is the girls-to-guy ratio is 10 to one.

The **Saw Mill Restaurant & Tavern** (1807 Boardwalk, 732/793-1990, www.sawmillcafe .com) is a boardwalk institution, and the best place in town to grab a slice of pizza—they're enormous! The restaurant has gone through numerous changes over the years, including an expansion (complete with a sushi bar) that some say makes the place less cozy, but it's still adequately loved. Upstairs is the 21-and-over **Green Room,** the town's best live-music venue. Theme nights include $2 Tijuana Tuesdays and Krazy Kup Thursdays, with $3 32-ounce beer refills all night long.

If a little respectability is what you're after, try **Klee's Bar and Grill** (101 Boulevard, 732/830-1996, www.kleesbarandgrill.com), an Irish pub offering a variety of casual eats, including pizza, burgers, and a house-made Klee's Pot Pie ($10.95). Live music is featured in the bar on weekends. Klee's **Next Door Cafe,** literally next door, serves breakfast (daily 7 A.M.–noon).

Getting There
Seaside Heights is located off Exit 82 of the Garden State Parkway.

ISLAND BEACH STATE PARK
One of New Jersey's most pristine coastal stretches, 3,003-acre Island Beach State Park (Seaside Park, 732/793-0506, www.njparks andforests.org/parks/island.html) hosts 10 miles of white-sand beaches, a wildlife preserve, natural trails, freshwater bogs, and maritime vegetation. Situated between the Atlantic Ocean and Barnegat Bay, this narrow barrier strip is a major stop along the Atlantic Flyway, a bird migration route, making it a hot spot for birders. The park is home to New Jersey's largest nesting osprey colony, and peregrine falcons, waterfowl, and warblers all travel through. Red foxes and turtles reside here, and additional seasonal visitors include butterflies, and in nearby waters, bluefish and striped bass. Island Beach is also a good spot to glimpse bottlenose dolphins during summer months, as well as the occasional harbor or gray seal (Dec.–Mar.).

The park has three sections: a northern natural area, a central recreational zone, and a southern natural area, containing the majority of the wildlife habitat. The northern zone's access is somewhat limited—it has been set aside as protected coastal habitat.

Sports and Recreation
There are eight less-than-a-mile-long nature trails scattered throughout the park, including one beginning from the central zone's year-round comfort station, and another leaving from the bird blind in the southern zone's Area 20. Interpretive exhibits along each trail offer insight into the park's natural and cultural offerings. Bicycle lanes run parallel to the road for cyclists. Horseback riding is permitted October–April on the six southernmost miles of Ocean Beach.

The park's central recreation zone features a mile-long beach designated for swimming, with lifeguards, a concession stand, first-aid station, and bathhouses open Memorial Day–Labor Day.

Scuba diving is permitted along a 2.5 mile stretch off the park's southern zone, beginning from Barnegat Inlet and heading north. Divers are required to first register with the park service. The southern tip of Ocean Bathing Area 3 in the central area is designated for surfing and windsurfing. Surfing is also allowed from Parking Area 2 south to the inlet.

Island Beach offers some of the Shore's best saltwater sportfishing—especially for striped bass and bluefish—and the southern tip of the park overlooking Barnegat Bay Lighthouse (the lighthouse is about an hour's drive, as access is limited to mainland routes) is reserved for fishing. Beach parking is allowed for those carrying permits; four-wheel drive is preferable. Sportfishing is also allowed at the central zone's Bathing Area 2 during the off-season.

The southern natural area also offers the park's best bird-watching ops (waterfowl are best sighted May–Oct.), as well as a boat launch for canoes and kayaks at Area 21. In summer, guided canoe and kayak excursions take place along Barnegat Bay, exploring the nearby Sedge Islands—a marine conservation zone where sighting may include nesting ospreys, falcons, and wading birds.

Daily educational programs are offered

throughout summer at Ocean Swimming Area 1. These may include all-age beach tours, fishing the Barnegat Bay, and learning about the local food chain. For an updated schedule, phone the park's nature center (732/793-1698).

Information and Services

Vehicle admission fees are $6 on weekdays, $10 on weekends Memorial Day–Labor Day, $5 daily in the off-season.

Island Beach offers selected tours and programs daily July–August, beginning from the central zone's First Pavilion visitors center at Ocean Bathing Area 1. For ranger assistance, call the park office (732/793-0506) or 911 in an emergency.

Public restrooms are scattered throughout the park, including at the park entryway, in the middle and southern portions of the central recreation zone, and in numerous spots along the southern natural area. A year-round facility is located at Lot A-7 in the central recreation zone, which also hosts a wooden walkway to the sea suitable for visitors with disabilities. Big-wheel rolling chairs are available at the central zone's Ocean Bathing Areas 1 and 2 pavilions during summer, and from the park service (offices are located between the two beaches) in the off-season.

Beach picnicking with grills is allowed in the central zone south of the designated swimming area. Picnickers must supply their own grills.

Long Beach Island and Vicinity

Long Beach Island, also known as LBI, is a thin barrier island stretching for 18 miles along the Jersey coast, with only one access bridge. The island is made up of several distinct towns, each attracting a different type of visitor. While LBI was once notorious for its dangerous coastal waters and the dozens of shipwrecks because of them, the island has more recently become known as "New Jersey's Hamptons," with parts of the island now appealing to vacationers used to trendy restaurants and boutique hotels. You can still find casual cedar shacks, surfing enclaves, campy eateries, and family-oriented entertainment throughout the island, and it's all brought together by one long boulevard.

Due to LBI's length and its lack of roadways and access points, traffic backs up easily. It's best to book a room in or near the island's region you plan on exploring; otherwise you'll spend much of your vacation in the car. The towns mentioned below run north–south along LBI.

There are several camping resorts and worthwhile attractions along the mainland's Route 9, just over the island's causeway bridge. It's a beautiful region and much more low-key than LBI during summer months. You might consider staying at one of the campgrounds

and driving over to LBI in the morning or afternoon.

Getting There

To reach Long Beach Island take Exit 63 off the Garden State Parkway. There's only one bridge to LBI.

BARNEGAT LIGHT

Other than its southern tip, Barnegat Light is probably Long Beach Island's least inhabited stretch. Situated at the top of the island across the inlet from Island Beach State Park, Barnegat Light (separate from the mainland's Barnegat Township) has a population of less than 1,000 and is smaller than one square mile in size. It's home to one of New Jersey's most photographed structures.

◖ Barnegat Lighthouse State Park

Thirty-two-acre Barnegat Lighthouse State Park (Barnegat Light, 609/494-2016, www .state.nj.us/dep/parksandforests/parks/barnlig .html, daily dawn–dusk), sits along LBI's northern tip, where the Atlantic Ocean and Barnegat Bay meet. It's a picturesque place

© LAURA KINIRY

Old Barney, the Barnegat lighthouse

filled with long sandy stretches and a maritime forest, as well as an interpretive center, a maritime forest nature trail, and plenty of waterfront property. Along the inlet separating Barnegat from Island Beach State Park (a few hundred yards by sea, an hour by car) is a 1,033-foot concrete walkway ideal for strolling, and often used by fishers casting for bluefish, weakfish, and flounder. The park is a popular spot for wildlife viewing, and seasonal birds are regular visitors. Waterfowl appear during summer shoulder seasons, shorebirds arrive for the high season, and warblers make their way through in fall. December–March it's possible to sight gray and harbor seals along Barnegat beaches. Thousands of monarch butterflies find temporary shelter in the maritime forest in late summer and early autumn. The park does not offer a public beach.

Barnegat is home to one of the state's most beloved lighthouses, a 172-foot, 217-step, red-and-white structure affectionately known as **Old Barney** (daily 9 A.M.–4:30 P.M. Memorial Day–Labor Day, Wed.–Sun. 9 A.M.–3:30 P.M.

Labor Day–Memorial Day, $1). Said to be New Jersey's most photographed lighthouse, Barney was erected in the 1850s when sailors complained its predecessor could be mistaken for a passing ship. Today, visitors can climb to the top of Barney's deactivated light tower for spectacular 360-degree views. Not to worry—numerous exhibit rooms serve as rest areas for those ascending (and descending) the spiral stairs.

Viking Village

Founded in the 1920s by Norwegian fishermen and renamed in 1972, Viking Village (19th St. and Bayview Ave., 609/494-0113) is home to a small row of shanty-style shops, including antiques purveyor **The Sea Wife** (609/361-8039, www.theseawife.com), and **Viking Outfitters** (609/361-9111), a clothing store for sea captains. Thirty-eight boats dock at Viking Village, which is one of the East Coast's largest fresh-fish suppliers, producing $25 million worth of seafood products annually. In conjunction with the Southern Ocean County Chamber of Commerce the village offers free dock tours Fridays at 10 A.M. throughout summer.

A bit of local trivia: Viking Village is home to the *Lindsay L* fishing vessel, which portrayed the *Hanna Bodan* in the 2000 movie *The Perfect Storm.*

Beaches

The best beach access in Barnegat Light is below 20th Street. Beach tags run $5 daily, $20 weekly, and $35 for the season. Those age 12 and under don't require beach tags. Beach wheelchairs are available for rent at Borough Hall (10 W. 10th St., 609/494-9196), and there's handicap parking at Ninth and 29th Streets. There are public restrooms at Barnegat Lighthouse State Park and at 10th Street and Bayview Avenue. Food and alcohol are permitted on the beach.

Accommodations

Tucked along a side road near Barnegat Lighthouse State Park is **Sand Castle** (710 Bayview Ave., 609/494-6555 or 800/253-0353, www.sandcastlelbi.com, $295–425), a modern luxury B&B best suited for couples. Five guest rooms and two suites come equipped with private baths, fireplaces, and a TV and DVD player, and each has its own private entry. Guests get complimentary use of the inn's bicycles—perfect for working off the gourmet breakfast served each morning. Added perks include a heated pool and a rooftop deck.

Food and Nightlife

On the far side of the lighthouse parking lot is **Kelly's Old Barney Restaurant** (3rd St. and Broadway, 609/494-5115, $6–11), a cozy nautically themed restaurant serving a simple menu of American eats like burgers, fries, and grilled cheese on white bread. Prices are reasonable, and there's outdoor seating in back. Kelly's is cash-only and is open seasonally.

Moustache Bill's Diner (8th and Broadway, 609/494-0155, $7–15) is an island favorite, an old-school diner crowded with locals and shoobies who pack in for pancakes, omelets, and grilled Reuben sandwiches. Open for breakfast and lunch only, hours are Thursday–Monday 6 A.M.–3 P.M., Tuesday–Wednesday 6 A.M.– 11:30 A.M. June–September, and Friday– Sunday 6 A.M.–3 P.M. during the off-season. The diner is closed January–mid-March.

Viking Village's **Viking Fresh Off the Hook** (1905 Bayview Ave., 609/361-8900, www.vikingoffthehook.com, call for hours, $6.95– 24.95) lives up to its name, selling deliciously straight-from-the-boat seafood (you can actually watch it coming ashore) accompanied by fries, slaw, or smashed potatoes. Hours vary throughout the year.

HARVEY CEDARS AND LOVELADIES

Harvey Cedars began as a whaling station, though today it's a mostly residential ocean and bayside community hosting a couple of excellent dining options. Its neighbor Loveladies is part of the larger Long Beach Township, a conglomeration of island communities scattered along LBI. Loveladies is named for Thomas Lovelady, a local man who owned a nearby island in the late 19th century. The neighborhood suffered considerable damage during LBI's infamous 1962 three-day storm, with many of its homes destroyed completely. They've since been rebuilt bigger and better, raised high on pilings and blocking beach views. You'll still see the occasional single-story home in Loveladies, but it's rare. As one of the island's thinnest portions, Loveladies doesn't have much to offer visitors, and public beach access is limited. While Loveladies is completely without restaurants, there are a couple of excellent dining options in Harvey Cedars. Overnight accommodations are hard to come by in both towns—try Barnegat Light to the north, or if you're up for a drive, head south about 13 miles to LBI's Beach Haven, home to the island's best lodging selection. Several worthwhile stays are scattered in between.

Beaches

Harvey Cedars offers both ocean and bay beaches. Daily tags for use at both cost $6, free for those age 12 and under. Restrooms are located at the bayfront **Sunset Park** (W. Salem Ave.) along with volleyball and boccie courts, a baseball field, and a paved fitness track. There's a beach access ramp for disabled people at Mercer Avenue and 80th Street, along with handicap parking. Beach surf chairs for those with limited mobility are available through the local borough (609/361-9733). There's a children's beach at 77th Street and the bay.

Loveladies beach is $5 daily, free for those under age 12 and over 65. Much of Loveladies' shoreline is considered private. Public access points are located in only a handful of spots, including Coast Avenue, Loveladies Lane, and Seashell Lane. Loveladies's public restrooms are located at Harbor South.

Events

The **Long Beach Island Foundation of the Arts and Sciences** (609/494-1241, www.lbifoundation.org) hosts an annual August **Seashore Open House Tour** ($30) featuring some of Loveladies's finest homes. A summer concert series is held Wednesday summer evenings at Harvey Cedars's **Sunset Park** (W. Salem Ave.) on the bay.

Food

LBI has earned the nickname "New Jersey's Hamptons" thanks in part to restaurants like **Plantation** (7908 Long Beach Blvd., Harvey Cedars, 609/494-8191, www.plantation restaurant.com, lunch daily 11:30 A.M.–2:30 P.M., dinner Sun.–Thurs. 4:30–9:30 P.M., Fri.–Sat. 4:30–10:30 P.M., $10–25), a Key West–inspired year-round eatery specializing in rum-infused drinks and contemporary fusion dishes, like Brazilian fish and chips with paprika fries ($23) and wasabi-crusted Chilean sea bass ($36). The refined island decor is much more Bogie and Bacall than Monchichi.

Next door is the informal **Harvey Cedars Shellfish Company** (7904 Long Beach Blvd., 609/494-7112, harveycedarsshellfishco.com), a BYO seafood market with picnic tables for dining that has been in business since 1976. The Company opens at 4:30 P.M. nightly during summer, with limited hours during off-season.

SURF CITY

Tiny Surf City—it covers less than one square mile—has a wonderful laissez-faire quality. Filled with residential shacks and casual eateries, you'll feel perfectly at home in flip-flops and T-shirt attire toting a board on the back of your bike.

Beaches

Beach tags cost $8 daily (under age 12 and over 65 free). Surf City's designated surfing beach is between North First and North Third Streets; its designated fishing beach is North 23rd–North 25th Streets. A bayside bathing beach exists near 15th Street and Barnegat Avenue. Beaches can be accessed from any side street. Public restrooms are located at **Borough Hall** (813 Long Beach Blvd., 609/494-3064).

Sports and Recreation

For surrey and bicycle rentals try **Surf Buggy Center** (1414 Long Beach Blvd., 609/361-3611), and for miniature golf, **Surf City Island**

Golf (603 Long Beach Island Blvd., 609/494-1709, $4–5). Surf City has a **surf-only beach** between First and Second Streets—look for the flags. Local bait and tackle shop **Surf City Bait & Tackle** (317 Long Beach Blvd., 609/494-2333) is one of many island shops selling clamming licenses.

Accommodations, Food, and Nightlife

One of LBI's oldest hotels, the **Surf City Hotel** (8th St. and Long Beach Island Blvd., 609/494-7281, www.surfcityhotel.com, $160–230) is a massive white clapboard practically swelling with salty air. In addition to air-conditioned rooms, each with a TV and a fridge, and a disability-equipped cottage, the hotel houses a pub, adjacent liquor store, restaurant, and even a clam bar. While live entertainment plays most summer evenings and Sunday afternoons, it's the hotel's happy hour that draws the most varied clientele, including New York City commuters and sock-and-sandal-clad shoobies. Before leaving, pick up a logo-topped sun visor at the hotel's souvenir stand.

For a breakfast that satisfies, try the year-round **Scojo's** (307 N. Long Beach Blvd., 609/494-8661, $7–14), also open for lunch and dinner.

SHIP BOTTOM AND LONG BEACH TOWNSHIP

Long Beach Township comprises a number of smaller areas, including Brant Beach (south of Ship Bottom), Spray Beach, Brighton Beach, and Beach Haven North. Ship Bottom is the island's centermost borough, the place where Route 72 drops you onto LBI. For this reason, Ship Bottom is more commercial than the rest of the island, and it lacks the community feel you'll find in other boroughs. Businesses have popped up sporadically along the wide main street, catering to summer's inevitable weekend traffic.

Beaches

Long Beach Township's daily beach tags cost $5 daily, $20 weekly, and $35 for the season;

Ship Bottom's are $7 daily, $17 weekly, and $35 for the season. Public restrooms are located within Ship Bottom's Borough Hall (1621 Long Beach Blvd., 609/494-2171), 10–12th Streets at the bay, and Branch Beach's Bayview Park (68th St.). Many of Ship Bottom's beaches are wheelchair-accessible. Alcohol is permitted on both beaches.

Sports and Recreation

One of the Mid-Atlantic coast's largest windsurfing shops, **Island Surf & Sail** (3304 Long Beach Blvd., Brant Beach, 609/494-5553, www.islandsurf-sail.com) rents wakeboard, windsurfing, and surfing equipment, and offers lessons in all three, along with kiteboarding (check the website for prices). Kayaks are also available.

Opened in the 1950s as a tiny local surf shop, Ship's Bottom's **Ron Jon Surf Shop** (201 W. 9th St., 609/494-8844, www.ronjons.com) has morphed into a glossy national retail franchise. Island old-timers who haven't visited recently won't recognize the flagship store—looming large like Oz at the causeway entry. LBI's original still sells boards, gear, and hip summer fashions, but if history is what you're after, it's buried beneath the jams and T-shirts.

Accommodations, Food, and Nightlife

Located at the base of the island's entry bridge, BYO **La Spiaggia** (357 W. 8th St., 609/494-4343, www.laspiaggialbi.com, $25–38) offers upscale Italian eats and outstanding service, a few steps above your typical Jersey Shore dining experience. With this in mind it's best to forgo the tank tops and flip-flops for more appropriate attire. The restaurant is open for dinner only, Tuesday–Sunday from 5 P.M. during summer, Wednesday–Sunday spring and fall; call for winter hours.

A local institution for half a century, **Joe Pop's Shore Bar** (2002 Long Beach Blvd., 609/494-0558, www.joepops.com, daily) is the island spot for seeing area bands like Big Orange Cone, Steamroller Picnic, and the loveable Nerds. In addition to nightly drink specials, the bar serves an extensive menu of simple American eats. Call ahead for off-season and exact hours.

Literally the first thing you see when arriving on Long Beach Island is the octagonal **Quarter Deck** (351 W. 9th St., 609/494-9055), a massive nightclub, restaurant, and motel combo with an outdoor deck and karaoke on weekends. Live music includes the Springsteen tribute band B-Street, and Vanilla Ice (ice baby).

Long Beach Island's first boutique hotel and restaurant, **Daddy O** (4401 Long Beach Blvd., 609/494-1300, www.daddyohotel.com, $235–325 s, $275–425 d) opened in August 2006 to rave reviews. Occupying the site and structure of a former 80-year-old hotel, this deceivingly retro clapboard and cedar space features 22 modern guest rooms on its second and third floors, and a New American bar and eatery beneath. Doused in deep browns and whites, rooms are small but stylish, and each comes equipped with halogen reading lamps, a flat-screen TV, and access to the rooftop deck, which also hosts private parties. Daddy O's sleek dining establishment (daily 11:30 A.M.–2:30 P.M., dinner daily from 4 P.M.) offers alfresco seating during warmer months (both the hotel and restaurant are open year-round) and an island-inspired menu of dishes, including pan-seared mahimahi ($26), and lump crab cakes with shoestring fries ($25).

BEACH HAVEN

Toward LBI's southern tip is Beach Haven, a predominantly residential borough hosting the island's only amusement pier. The Haven includes a small historic district with a museum and dozens of century-old cedar Victorians, as well as a wonderful local theater and adjoining ice cream parlor. Keeping with its family image, the borough has a strict 11 P.M. curfew for minors.

Sights

For more than a quarter century **Fantasy Island Amusement Park** (320 W. 7th St., 609/492-4000, www.fantasyislandpark.com) has been entertaining LBI visitors. Enjoy a bird's-eye view aboard the Ferris wheel, get queasy on the swinging Sea Dragon, or sit cozy on the carousel. Later, test your eye at an old-school shooting gallery before gorging on funnel cake and soft-serve cones. An indoor casino arcade features hundreds of slot machines, skee-ball courts, and giant crane games. Cash in your ticket wins for some of the best arcade prizes along the shore. Fifteen bucks will get you a roll of twenty tokens, and most rides require 3–5. The park opens Saturday–Thursday at 6 P.M., Fridays at 2 P.M. throughout summer. The arcade opens at noon.

Stop by the **Long Beach Island Museum** (Engleside and Beach Aves., 609/492-0700, www.lbi.net/nonprof/lbimusm.html, $3 donation) to get an understanding of island history, including information on its whaling community beginnings and details on the three-day storm of 1962, which destroyed a large percentage of the island's homes and forever altered its physical geography. The museum provides self-guided tour brochures for Beach Haven's historic district, and hosts guided

neighborhood tours ($8) throughout summer. Hours are weekends 2–4 P.M. May–June and early September, daily 10 A.M.–4 P.M. July and August. They're also open Tuesdays year-round; just knock on the back door.

The **Edwin B. Forsythe National Wildlife Refuge's Holgate Unit** (www.fws.gov/north east/forsythe/), an endangered piping plover nesting site, occupies LBI's southern tip. It's open for visits during nonnesting season (Sept.–Mar.), and is the perfect place for a quiet beach stroll.

Beaches

Beach Haven's beach access costs $5 daily, $15 weekly, and $25 for the season. Beaches can be accessed from anywhere, but Centre Street Beach has a wheelchair ramp. Restrooms are available at Centre Street and Dock Road, Schooner's Wharf, and in the Bay Village shopping area. Alcohol and picnics are prohibited on the beach, though it's alright to bring along a small sandwich.

A special toddler beach is located on the bay at Taylor Avenue, where there's also a playground and basketball courts.

Entertainment

Home to Ocean County's only professional theater, Beach Haven's beloved **Surflight Theatre** (Engleside and Beach Aves., 609/492-9477 or 609/492-4469, www.surflight.org, $29 adult, $9 child) has been running musical and stage productions such as *Kismet, Mister Roberts,* and *Oklahoma!* for more than 50 years. The theater has 450 seats, and performances—including children's theater ($9)—run throughout summer and fall, as well as the December holiday season.

True theater fans start the night at next door's **Show Place Ice Cream Parlor** (200 Centre St., Beach Haven, 609/492-0018, www.surflight.org/showplac.htm, daily from 6 P.M. summer), an old-fashioned ice cream parlor with checkered floors, candy-striped walls, and fabulous themed specialties like the Phantom of the Opera chocolate sundae, topped with a mask of marshmallow. But the best part about

© LAURA KINIRY

Beach Haven's historic district

THE SHORE'S BACK ROUTE

Between the Shore's barrier islands and the mainland, beginning south from the Manasquan River, lie a series of salt water bays, natural inlets, rivers, and manmade canals connecting all the way to Texas. Called the **Intracoastal Waterway**, this Congress-authorized stretch acts as a toll-free route protecting boats from Atlantic seas and storms. New Jersey's portion, a back-bay wonderland bordering Route 9, often goes undiscovered. Here are some of its local roadside highlights:

HURRICANE HOUSE

An area institution, the Hurricane House (688 East Bay Ave., Barnegat, 609/698-5040, Mon.-Fri. 11 A.M.-10 P.M., Sat.-Sun. 7 A.M.-10 P.M.) has an interesting history. Originally built as a Victorian home, the property became a pool hall in 1918 after a fire destroyed the original structure. By 1920 it was a general store, morphing into the Hurricane House restaurant sometime in the 1970s. The business eventually closed, only to reopen as a restaurant and ice cream parlor in 2001. Recently, the Hurricane House underwent a complete interior renovation. Burgundy walls, high-backed booths, and a piano (and player) have been added, bringing back the establishment's original look and feel. Casual American eats (and ice cream) are served throughout the day.

TUCKERTON SEAPORT VILLAGE

Across Little Egg Harbor from Long Beach Island is 40-acre Tuckerton Seaport (120 W. Main St., 609/296-8868, www.tuckertonseaport.org, $8 adult, $3 child 6-12), a restored living-history village and New Jersey's only one dedicated to maritime culture. Opened in 2000, Tuckerton Seaport has all the makings of an authentic seaport village: docks, decoy carvers, and boat builders, along with 16 waterfront buildings. There's even a lighthouse, modeled after one that originally stood on Tucker's Island, off Long Beach Island's southern tip, but was washed away in a 1927 storm. The seaport is home to the **Jacques Cousteau National Estuarine Research Center,** hosting a visitors center and public maritime exhibits. And if traffic along Route 9 is too backed up, you can always arrive by boat.

Tuckerton Seaport Village is open daily 10 A.M.-5 P.M. during summer, Friday-Sunday 11 A.M.-4 P.M. in the off-season.

CAPTAIN MIKE'S MARINA

Located along Great Bay Boulevard just south of Tuckerton Seaport, Mike's (fourth bridge along Great Bay Blvd., 609/296-4406, www.captmikesmarina.com) was established in 1937 and serves as the region's premier place for boat and kayak rentals. Choose among 16- to 19-foot Carolina skiffs, wooden garveys, and 18-foot Pontoon boats. Prices range $75-190 for weekday boat rentals, and $25 for a two-hour single kayak rental. Guided kayaking tours ($45 per person, Wed. and Fri.) teach about the local habitat by taking participants through the marshes and wetlands. The area is popular with birds – you may even see nesting ospreys. Reservations for boat rentals and tours are strongly recommended.

Mike's is also home to a full-service bait and tackle shop, dry storage, and boat ramps.

OYSTER CREEK INN

Oyster Creek Inn (41 N. Oyster Creek Rd., 609/652-8565, Tues.-Sat. 4-9 P.M., Sun. 1-9 P.M. summer, $15-27) is an old-style fish house located along the back roads of Leeds Point and is an experience beyond the food (which is superb). The cedar-shake building that the restaurant and bar occupy is among two dozen such residential and fishing shacks situated along the area's back-bay marshlands, and the inn's outdoor deck is perfect for idling time while watching boats slip upstream. Oyster Creek's interior hosts familiar wood-paneled walls, with oyster crackers and horseradish atop every checkered-cloth table. The restaurant is known for its seafood: fried, grilled, broiled, and cooked to perfection. The casual Crab Room serves drinks and a raw bar menu. Get here early; reservations aren't accepted.

this place is its singing teenage staff, whose framed photos hang at the entrance. Donning the outfits of a barbershop quartet, they provide both double scoops and double octaves, and it's almost required that someone in your party join in the fun.

Shopping

Shoppers will want to check out Beach Haven's **Bay Village and Schooners Wharf** (9th St. between Ocean and Bay Aves., on the bay, 609/492-2800), an open-air multilevel shopping village with a wood-shingled seafaring theme. Shop for pajamas aboard an old sea schooner, or peruse for kites, candy, and ecofriendly gifts.

Sports and Recreation

LBI's double-decker paddlewheel *Crystal Queen* riverboat (Centre St. and Bayfront, 609/822-8849 or 609/492-0333 in-season, www.blackwhalecruises.com, May–Oct.) offers sightseeing cruises along Little Egg Harbor Bay and day trips to Atlantic City. One-hour evening bay cruises take place daily at 7 P.M. and 8:30 P.M. July–September.

Seasonal **Thundering Surf Waterpark** (Taylor and Bay Aves., 609/492-0869, www .thunderingsurfwaterpark.com, daily 9 A.M.– 7:30 P.M. July–Aug., $21.95 for two hours) is home to six giant waterslides, dancing fountains, a lazy "crazy" river, and the kiddie play land Cowabunga Beach. When you're ready to dry off, head over to the adjacent **Settler's Mill Adventure Golf** (daily 9 A.M.–11 P.M. July–Aug.), two 18-hole miniature golf courses ($7.50 and $9.95), both with a maritime theme. Call ahead for June and September hours.

Local water sports include **Beach Haven Parasailing** (2702 Long Beach Blvd., 609/492-0375, www.bhparasail.com), sportfishing with **June Bug Charters** (Beach Haven Yacht Club, Engleside Ave. at the bay, 856/778-0200 or 609/685-2839 cell, www .fish-junebug.com) or **L.B.I. Fishing Charters** (Morrison's Beach Haven Marina, 2nd St. and the bay, 609/492-2591, www.lbifishing charters.com), and **kayak rentals** from

Holgate Marina (83 Tebco Terr., 609/492-0191), just south of Beach Haven.

Founded in 1987, LBI's **Alliance for a Living Ocean** (2007 Long Beach Blvd., 609/492-0222, www.livingocean.org) promotes understanding and protection of the local aquatic ecosystem. In addition to various educational and craft programs offered for adults and kids throughout summer, the alliance hosts three-hour ecotours around the bay on select days July–August; call for details.

Accommodations

Beach Haven's historic district is home to the borough's B&Bs, along with a couple of worthwhile motels.

The **Victoria Guest House** (126 Amber St., 609/492-4154, www.lbivictoria.com, $220–265 s, $235–280 d) offers spacious period-themed rooms—many with four-poster beds—at one of two side-by-side locations, depending on the time of year. Both homes are less than a one-block walk to the beach and include wireless Internet, home-baked goods, and private baths. The summer home also allows use of an in-ground pool.

Don't let the updated Victorian exterior fool you; **Julia's of Savannah** (209 Centre St., 609/492-5004, www.juliasoflbi.com, $260–325) is plentiful with antiques. Air-conditioned rooms are small but cared for, with beds that make you want to stay put. Amenities include private baths and a full breakfast, and a lovely wraparound porch that catches the sea breeze. A first-floor room with a private porch is available for guests with disabilities.

Rooms at the beachfront **Engleside Inn** (Engleside Ave. at the oceanfront, 609/492-1251 or 800/762-2214, www.engleside.com, $244–365 s, $290–446 d) are spacious, if not a bit dated, ranging in size from single motel rooms to two-room efficiencies. Ocean views are prominent in many of the larger rooms. The inn hosts its own outdoor beach bar secluded by dunes, as well as a sushi bar and the highly rated Leeward Room, an American fine-dining restaurant.

Food

Stop into **Slice of Heaven** (610 N. Bay Ave., 609/492-7437, $3–20) for a slice of cheese steak–topped pizza, or order an entire pie— the baked ziti pie rocks. Friday and Saturday evening hours extend until 4 A.M. during summer.

Not sure what to have for breakfast? At the pig-themed **Uncle Will's Pancake House** (3 S. Bay Ave., 609/492-2514, daily 7 A.M.–1 P.M., dinner Thurs.–Sun. 5–9 P.M., summer) you'll have your pick. A local institution, Uncle Will's conjures up creative morning meals like peach pancake platters and stuffed French toast, and if you're lucky, serves them along with a ceramic pig that'll stay by your side as you eat. Caribbean-inspired dinners ($17–25) are also worth a try.

The seasonal **Chicken or the Egg** (207 N. Bay Ave., 609/492-3695, www.492fowl.com, daily 24/7 summer, $6–10) dishes out a full diner-style menu of breakfasts, sandwiches, soups, salads, and platters. Large wood booths act as hidden havens during early mornings, when locals scarf down peanut-butter-cup pancakes and egg sandwiches following late nights at the bar. Decor is—you guessed it—poultry themed.

Long a foodie favorite, **The Gables** (212 Centre St., 609/492-3553, www.gableslbi.com, daily 9 A.M.–3 P.M. and 5:30–10 P.M. summer, Fri.–Sat. 9 A.M.–3 P.M. and 5:30–10 P.M. off-season, closed Jan.) came under new ownership in 2005, opening a year later better than ever. The restaurant occupies the former dining room in a century-old home, just downstairs from a B&B. Romance is everywhere, from the dining room's wood-burning fireplace to its candlelit tables and original wood plank floors. Guests can also dine or sip tea in an outdoor Victorian garden, surrounded by flowers and a bubbling fountain. The eclectic menu features both prix fixe and à la carte selections that change daily, but may include dishes like handmade potato gnocchi and butter-poached Maine lobster.

MAINLAND
Camping

While no camping facilities exist on LBI, there are a few mainland resorts close enough to be considered overnight alternatives.

Family operated for more than 40 years, **Baker's Acres Campground** (230 Willets Ave., Parkertown, 609/296-2664 or 800/648-2227, www.bakersacres.com, May–Nov.) features 300 shaded sites set along the eastern edge of the Pinelands. The campground also hosts two in-ground pools, and offers hot showers and volleyball nets for play. Rentable cabins and cottages have recently been added. Sites cost $34–44 a night depending on amenities.

Approximately eight miles west of LBI, **Sea Pirate Family Campground** (Rte. 9, West Creek, 609/296-7400, www.sea-pirate.com, May–Oct., $35–52) features an indoor-outdoor sports complex with Ping-Pong, a baseball diamond, and a basketball court, as well as motorboat and kayak rentals and annual events, such as July's '50s Night and Sock Hop, held throughout summer.

Atlantic City

The city that was once "America's Playground" is now "Always Turned On," at least according to its latest marketing campaign. Whatever the case, Atlantic City is one for the books. From its humble beginnings as a fly-infested sand dune little more than a century ago, the city has made a name for itself across the country and throughout the world. Atlantic City may call to mind images that aren't always good, but this beachfront property is responsible for much of the Americana we know and love: Miss America, boardwalks, Monopoly, amusement piers, and supposedly even saltwater taffy. From the Rat Pack to the crack pack, Vanessa Williams to the Donald, Atlantic City has seen it all. Its history is dotted with diving

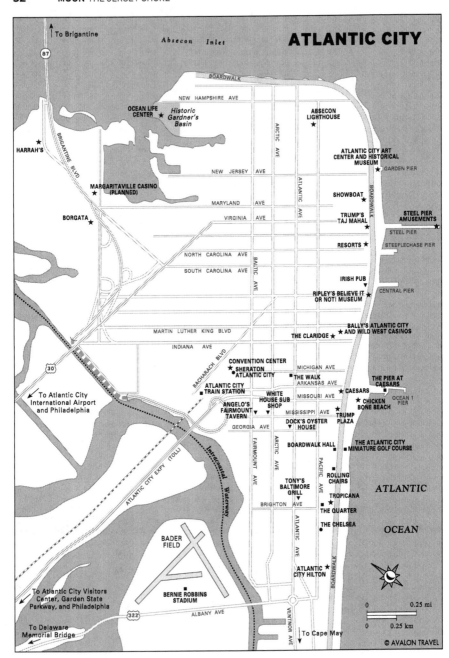

ATLANTIC CITY

To Brigantine

Absecon Inlet

BOARDWALK

NEW HAMPSHIRE AVE

OCEAN LIFE CENTER ★ Historic Gardner's Basin

ABSECON LIGHTHOUSE ★

ARCTIC AVE

HARRAH'S ★

BRIGANTINE BLVD

NEW JERSEY AVE

ATLANTIC AVE

ATLANTIC CITY ART CENTER AND HISTORICAL MUSEUM

GARDEN PIER

MARGARITAVILLE CASINO (PLANNED) ★

MARYLAND AVE

SHOWBOAT ★

BOARDWALK

BORGATA ★

VIRGINIA AVE

TRUMP'S TAJ MAHAL ★

STEEL PIER AMUSEMENTS ★

STEEL PIER

RESORTS ★

STEEPLECHASE PIER

NORTH CAROLINA AVE

SOUTH CAROLINA AVE

BALTIC AVE

IRISH PUB ▼

CENTRAL PIER

RIPLEY'S BELIEVE IT OR NOT! MUSEUM ★

MARTIN LUTHER KING BLVD

BALLY'S ATLANTIC CITY ★ AND WILD WEST CASINOS

INDIANA AVE

THE CLARIDGE ★

BACHARACH BLVD

To Atlantic City International Airport and Philadelphia

30

CONVENTION CENTER ★ SHERATON ATLANTIC CITY

MICHIGAN AVE

THE WALK ■

ARKANSAS AVE

THE PIER AT CAESARS ■

ATLANTIC CITY TRAIN STATION ■

WHITE HOUSE SUB SHOP ■

MISSOURI AVE

CAESARS ★

OCEAN 1 PIER

ANGELO'S FAIRMOUNT TAVERN ▼

MISSISSIPPI AVE

CHICKEN BONE BEACH ●

TRUMP PLAZA ★

GEORGIA AVE

DOCK'S OYSTER HOUSE ▼

Intracoastal Waterway

ATLANTIC CITY EXPY (TOLL)

FAIRMOUNT AVE

ARCTIC AVE

BOARDWALK HALL ■

THE ATLANTIC CITY ■ MINIATURE GOLF COURSE

PACIFIC AVE

ROLLING CHAIRS ●

ATLANTIC

TONY'S BALTIMORE GRILL ▼

TROPICANA ★

BRIGHTON AVE

ATLANTIC AVE

THE QUARTER ●

OCEAN

BADER FIELD

THE CHELSEA ●

To Atlantic City Visitors Center, Garden State Parkway, and Philadelphia

ATLANTIC CITY HILTON ★

BOARDWALK

BERNIE ROBBINS STADIUM ■

To Delaware Memorial Bridge

322

ALBANY AVE

VENTNOR AVE

To Cape May

0   0.25 mi

0   0.25 km

© AVALON TRAVEL

horses and Chicken Bone beaches, historic hotels and a Steel Pier that just won't quit.

After decades of decline, Atlantic City seems to be regaining some of its groove. Over the last ten years the city has added boutique shopping centers and killer spas, a casino that rivals Vegas, and some of the best new restaurants in the state, all the while holding onto many of the establishments that once made it one of the country's top seaside resorts. Some complain that AC is pulling a Vegas with its swanky stores, open-air bars, and attempts to become a foodie destination, but why shouldn't it? Vegas hasn't fared too poorly. Since the 2003 opening of the Borgata Resort, the city that for years drew almost exclusively senior citizens is again attracting the young—luring singles with top-shelf martini bars, tightly clad cocktail waitresses, and plenty of nightlife.

There's so much to do in Atlantic City and its surrounding region that it's worth sticking around a bit. When the buzz of computerized casino slots becomes unbearable there's always the Boardwalk, beach, and shops to explore, not to mention an awesome historical museum, a bayside village, minor-league baseball, a 65-foot-tall elephant, and nearby golf courses, wineries, and nature preserves. And that's if you're not hungry or in town for a festival or show. There's no shortage of hotel rooms and restaurants, but for the best dining, venture outside of the main casinos, where food tends to be overpriced and underwhelming. Cocktails are easy to come by any time of day or night.

History

When the first passenger train arrived in Atlantic City from Camden, New Jersey, on July 1, 1854, "America's Playground" was born. And the city spent no time messing around. AC grew quickly, both architecturally and population-wise. Taverns, boarding homes, and grand hotels sprang up throughout town. During the late 19th and early 20th centuries, Atlantic City was the place to be. The world's first boardwalk came into existence, and amusement piers appeared every few blocks. At Heinz Pier, H. J. Heinz (of ketchup fame) gave away free pickles and pickle lapel pins for 46 years, and the Million Dollar Pier entertained spectators with kangaroo boxing, magic performances by legendary magician Harry Houdini, and the famous High Diving Horse Act, featuring a woman and horse diving together from a 40-foot platform into a pool.

Unfortunately, by the mid-20th century, Atlantic City's heyday had ended. Its grand hotels had fallen into disrepair, and visitors were no longer coming. Looking for a way to improve their situation, city officials approved gambling in 1976. Atlantic City became the first U.S. location outside Las Vegas where a person could place a legal bet. As part of the agreement, all casinos had to include a hotel complex with at least 50 guest rooms. Revenue began pouring in. But what was happening behind the casino's windowless walls didn't reflect what was going on along Atlantic City's streets; life in Atlantic City hadn't improved. Under the Boardwalk a community of gamblers and addicts were establishing makeshift

a New Jersey original

© LAURA KINIRY

THE HOTTEST COMMODITY IN TOWN

Only one walkway holds the indubitable distinction of being named Boardwalk with a capital *B*: That is Atlantic City's Boardwalk, the first known creation of its kind. Originally built in 1870, its purpose was not a commercial endeavor but simply a way of preventing beach strollers from tracking sand into hotel lobbies and railway cars. The Boardwalk was the brainchild of Alexander Boardman, a railway conductor and owner of Atlantic City's Ocean House hotel. Concerned about the damage his hotel's fine furnishings were undergoing by the same people he was bringing to enjoy the Shore's amenities, Boardman and fellow proprietor Jacob Keim gathered local hotel owners to discuss the problem. Boardman suggested a "raised platform" where visitors could stroll while still viewing the ocean, and the idea was met with overwhelming approval. City council financed the project with $5,000 in redeemable scrip. On June 26, 1870, the world's first boardwalk opened to the public.

Made of wooden planks 1.5 inches thick, the original Boardwalk was 10 feet wide and pieced together in 12-foot sections, each board laid lengthwise 18 inches from the ground. Although not the most likely material for salty air and weather-beaten shores, the wooden planks had an obvious purpose: to be easily removed and stored away after each summer season. While this preserved them from the harsh winter elements, it didn't protect the boards from the masses of visitors they attracted, nearly twice the amount of vacationers Atlantic City had seen in the previous 16 years. Within 10 years the structure had worn thin, and a new boardwalk was built.

With this new boardwalk came relaxed commercial zoning. Previously restricted to thirty feet from the walkway, the Boardwalk's consumer potential could now be fully realized. Businesses jumped at the opportunity. As new establishments fought for space, two more walkways came and went, resulting in a fifth and final Boardwalk built in 1896. It was this Boardwalk – raised to five feet above ground, widened to 40 feet across, and attached to a steel bar base structure with hand

the Steel Pier along Atantic City's Boardwalk

railings (people were constantly falling off the boards onto the beach) – given the street name "Boardwalk." It's the same structure used today.

While Atlantic City's present-day fame comes from its role as Vegas on the beach, the Boardwalk enjoyed a heyday long before the casinos. The city brought amusement piers to life, and with them came variety shows and big-name acts like Harry Houdini and Abbott and Costello. The Boardwalk's first beauty pageant, originally held as a ploy to extend the summer season, paved the way for Atlantic City's long-running Miss America Pageant and Boardwalk Parade. The city built a five-block-long Convention Hall (now Boardwalk Hall) along the boards in 1929 to host the increasingly popular pageant festivities. It's also said the world's first saltwater taffy came into being here, "invented" by a candy store proprietor after a storm flooded his shop.

Perhaps the Boardwalk's most notable claim to fame is as the hottest property to land a top hat or thimble. In 1934 an unemployed man named Charles Darrow developed a board game to entertain his friends during their Depression-era woes. Atlantic City's actual streets and properties were chosen to decorate the board, with Boardwalk being the most lucrative square. The game's name? Monopoly.

homes, and crime still ran rampant across the Monopoly board. But inside, busloads of tourists were enjoying a world of free drinks, jingling shot machines, and all-you-can-eat buffets. To better understand how casinos have changed AC, consider this: The city's entire population is smaller than the number of people the casinos employ.

Atlantic City's rep became that of a day-tripper destination for senior citizens and a place for after-prom parties. And the city seemed content with this until the Borgata opened in 2003. Suddenly investors saw opportunity. Now there are worthwhile shops, exciting clubs, sleek restaurants, spas, and some wonderful new hotels spread throughout town. AC still has a long way to go toward adjusting its image and improving its streets, but it seems to be heading in the right direction.

For a better understanding of Atlantic City just before and after the casino boom, rent *The King of Marvin Gardens,* starring Jack Nicholson and Bruce Dean, and *Atlantic City,* with Susan Sarandon and Burt Lancaster. AC, exposed in all its urban-grit glory, plays a starring role in each.

THE BOARDWALK

Atlantic City's six-mile-long, 60-foot-wide Boardwalk with a capital *B* is both the world's first boardwalk and New Jersey's largest, brimming with casino arcades (and casinos), palm-reading stands, hourly massage houses, knickknack shops, a couple of amusement piers, and the obligatory T-shirt shops and greasy food pits. The Boardwalk's famed **Rolling Chairs,** large wicker seats on wheels pushed by chatty men and women willing to cart you wherever you like (for a fee), are everywhere. The cost of rides varies depending on the rolling chair company, but usually run about $5 (plus a tip) for the first five Boardwalk blocks, increasing in $5 increments for every five blocks after. Discounts are offered on half-hour and hour tours. Most chairs seat two and are cash-only. If you have the time and money, it's a worthwhile experience. Rolling chairs have been part of the local landscape for more than a century.

While no one is entirely sure where the name "saltwater taffy" came from, most people agree the confection was born in Atlantic City. Here on the boards there's no better place than **Fralinger's** (1325 Boardwalk, 609/344-0442), unless of course you're a longstanding fan of **James Salt Water Taffy** (1519 Boardwalk, 609/344-1519, www.jamescandy.com). Maybe you're more of a fudge person? Then **Steel's Fudge** (1633 Boardwalk, 609/345-4051, www.steelsfudge.com), in business on Atlantic City's Boardwalk since 1919, is your place.

Since Mr. Peanut is one of the city's unofficial mascots, it's only fitting that the walkway's numerous **Boardwalk Peanut Shoppes** (609/272-1511, www.boardwalkpeanuts.com) are favorites among visitors. Look for one in Resorts and Trump Plaza.

Though a popular Boardwalk attraction, the much-hyped **Ripley's Believe It or Not! Museum** (New York Ave. and Boardwalk, 609/347-2001, www.ripleys.com, daily 10 A.M.–10 P.M. May–Aug., Mon.–Fri. 10 A.M.–6 P.M., Sat.–Sun. 10 A.M.–8 P.M. Apr. and Sept., $15 adult, $10 child 5–12) is nothing if not touristy. If you miss it here you can catch the same sorts of oddities displayed in Orlando, Florida, or at San Francisco's Fisherman's Wharf.

Atlantic City Art Center and Historical Museum

Atlantic City has a varied and interesting history, and the best place to uncover it is the Atlantic City Historical Museum (New Jersey Ave. at Boardwalk, 609/347-5837, www.acmuseum.org, daily 10 A.M.–4 P.M., free), situated at the north end of the Boardwalk's commercial strip. Operating alongside the Atlantic City Art Center (both museums are free), the historical museum's permanent exhibit, "Atlantic City: Playground of the Nation," provides a great overview of the city's prosperous past, and there's a nice collection of Miss America memorabilia. The museum's newest exhibit, "Shore Deco: Atlantic City Design Between the Wars, 1919–1939," opened summer 2006. Museum visitors will receive a souvenir Heinz pickle pin, a replica of those handed out by H. J. Heinz himself at the Boardwalk's turn-of-the-20th-century Heinz Pier. The nearby AC Art Center features three exhibit galleries and a shop selling local work, including Wheaton Village glass.

Boardwalk Hall

Opened in 1929, Atlantic City's landmark Boardwalk Hall (2301 Boardwalk, 609/348-7000, www.boardwalkhall.com) played official host to the Miss America Pageant from 1933 until 2004, longer than any other venue. Although the pageant has since left town (and New Jersey), Boardwalk Hall remains a sought-after showcase, hosting high-profile concerts such as Van Halen's reunion tour, Jimmy Buffet, and Madonna, along with conferences year-round. Even if you're not in town for a concert or event, stop by the Hall to have a peek at the world's largest pipe organ, with over 33,000 pipes, built 1929–1932. Tours of the organ and a theater-type organ, located in Boardwalk Hall's ballroom, are given monthly by the Atlantic City Convention Hall Organ Society (www.acchos.org); visit their website for details.

Boardwalk Recreation

Directly across from Boardwalk Hall is **The Atlantic City Miniature Golf Course** (1 Kennedy Plaza, 609/347-1661, www.ac minigolf.com), home of the 2005 Harris Cup National Miniature Golf Championship. This 18-hole course was recently updated with new Astroturf and sand traps, providing it with a pro-golf feel and a steady flow of players on summer weekday afternoons.

A highlight of the year-round **Central Pier Arcade & Speedway** (St. James Pl. and Tennessee Ave., 609/345-5219) is its large selection of redemption arcade games, where players can rack up tickets to trade for prizes. The pier is also home to go-karts, and a "Shoot the Geek" paintball game that uses live targets.

Since 1898 the **Steel Pier** (Virginia Ave. and 1000 Boardwalk, 866/386-6659, www.steel pier.com, Mon.–Fri. 3 P.M.–midnight, Sat.–Sun. noon–1 A.M. mid-June–Aug., Sat.–Sun.

noon–1 A.M. May–mid-June and Sept.–Oct.) has been bringing the hordes to Atlantic City, and somehow it (thankfully) continues going strong. Its last year was supposed to be 2006, but the amusements have been given ongoing reprieve by the pier's owner, Donald Trump, who plans to eventually redevelop it with a hotel, condos, and restaurants. Ride the Giant Slide, fly up in a helicopter, and stare amazed at the Skycycle Trapeze—a couple performing motorcycle stunts on a 60-foot-high tightrope—while you still have the chance.

OTHER SIGHTS
Absecon Lighthouse

Absecon Lighthouse (31 S. Rhode Island Ave., 609/449-1360, www.absteconlighthouse.org, daily 10 A.M.–5 P.M. July–Aug., Thurs.–Mon. 11 A.M.–4 P.M. Sept.–June, $7 adult, $5 senior, $4 child) is New Jersey's tallest lighthouse and the country's third-tallest. For a glimpse of Atlantic City before gambling took over, even preceding its days as America's Playground, come here. The attractive 228-step structure was built in 1857 and still has its first-order Fresnel lens. In the late 1990s the lighthouse underwent major restorations and now includes a replica of the light keeper's house, a museum, and a gift shop.

Atlantic City Convention Center

Opened in May 1997, the **Atlantic City Convention Center** (1 Miss America Way, 609/449-2000, www.accenter.com) hosts many of the city's largest fairs and festivals, including the biannual antique and collectible fair Atlantique City, Atlantic City's Classic Car Show, and an annual beer festival. The center features five second-floor showrooms and more than 500,000 square feet of contiguous exhibit space, as well as its own Sheraton Hotel. It's located just off the Atlantic City Expressway next to the train and bus stations.

BEACHES

Atlantic City's beaches are free, no tags required. Alcohol is permitted on the beach. Public restrooms are located along the

Boardwalk at Bartram Avenue, Albany Avenue, Chelsea Avenue, Mississippi Avenue, New Jersey Avenue, New Hampshire Avenue, and Caspian Avenue. Changing stations are available at Albany Avenue and South Carolina Avenue. The casino beach bars have showers available for public access. To reserve a surf chair for those with limited mobility (access ramps exist at various points along the Boardwalk), call 609/347-5312.

The beach directly in front of Missouri Avenue and Boardwalk is known as **Chicken Bone Beach,** named for the thousands of African American families who vacationed here in the early 1900s with their chicken-filled picnic hampers. Rat Pack performer Sammy Davis Jr. would join them while in town. The Chicken Bone Beach Historical Foundation hosts free jazz concerts at Kennedy Plaza, between Mississippi and Georgia Avenues, throughout summer.

CASINOS

Most of Atlantic City's approximately dozen casinos are set along the Boardwalk, with a few located along the bay en route to Brigantine. The city doesn't have a lot of room left for construction, although the October 2007 Sands Casino implosion has left a gaping hole soon to be filled with a Pinnacle Entertainment megacasino.

Atlantic City's casinos are all-inclusive, 24-hour establishments where the sun don't shine and the customers don't quit till their pockets are empty. Each of the casino resorts offers hotel rooms, restaurants, lounges and bars, shops, live showcase theaters, nightclubs, and often arcades, along with slot machines, poker and blackjack tables, roulette wheels, keno, and private gambling rooms galore. Free drinks are usually available to anyone spending money on the casino floor. New Jersey's 21-and-over gambling laws are strictly enforced, and no one under 21 is even allowed on the casino floors. Underage visitors are, however, permitted in the hotels, restaurants, and shopping halls.

Each casino has its own parking garage. Spaces cost $4–7, but most garages will give you two receipts upon entry: one as proof of payment and the other to use for complimentary parking at a second casino. Don't hesitate to request a second receipt if you only receive one.

Most casinos offer some sort of VIP card with substantial room and food discounts depending on the amount of time and money you spend. If planning a trip to a particular casino, inquire about obtaining a card at the customer service desk.

Atlantic City's jitney bus service offers round-the-clock transport between the casinos, and it's a good option for getting from the Boardwalk to bayside casinos if you've arrived by train or simply prefer leaving your car parked. If you're sticking strictly to Boardwalk casinos, walking from beginning to end is a stretch but doable. Otherwise, the Boardwalk Rolling Chairs offer a memorable alternative. A little-used walkway connects the three bayside casinos.

Borgata

The cream of Atlantic City's casino crop and also the latest edition to its skyline, the bayside Borgata is most responsible for glamming up AC and attracting younger crowds. If this is the city's fountain of youth, than water's flowing from every Chihuly-blown chandelier hanging in the casino's entryways. Scantily clad Borgata Babes deliver drinks on the casino floor, and surrounding the slots and game tables are high-end boutiques, decadent restaurants, and some of the hottest bars in town.

The 1,100-seat **Music Box** (800/736-1420) is Borgata's intimate live showcase, a great place for catching a performance by Alanis Morissette or Herbie Hancock. For more of a stadium crowd, check out Bob Dylan or the Black Crowes at the 30,000-square-foot **Event Center.** As casinos go, the Borgata's got some of the best restaurants of any in town. Fine dining establishments include **Ombra** (Tues.–Thurs. and Sun. 5–10 P.M., Fri.–Sat. 5–11 P.M., $20–38) famous for its wines (over 14,000 bottles) and cheeses; **Bobby Flay Steak** (Mon.–Thurs. 5–11 P.M., Fri.–Sat. 5 P.M.–midnight, Sun. 4–11 P.M., $29–50), the Food Network personality's first-ever steakhouse; and **Old**

Homestead (Mon.–Thurs. 5–11 P.M., Fri.–Sat. 5 P.M.–midnight, Sun. 4–11 P.M.), purveyor of the 20-ounce Kobe burger ($41). For something more affordable try a wood-oven pizza ($13–16) from **Wolfgang Puck Tavern** (Wed.–Mon. 5–11 P.M., closed Tues.) or **Bread + Butter** (Sun.–Thurs. 7 A.M.–10 P.M., Fri.–Sat. 7 A.M.–4 A.M.), offering white-bread sandwiches like portobello and provolone ($7.50) and pepperoni and American cheese ($7.50) that don't break the bank. Reservations for each can be made by calling 866/692-6742.

Curtains are all that separate 24-hour **B Bar** from the casino floor action, so for something more exclusive check out **Mixx** (Fri.–Sat. 10 P.M.–till the party's over,) a dimly lit dance club with a DJ spinning world beats.

Harrah's

Standing just before the Brigantine Bridge in Atlantic City's Marina District, Harrah's (777 Harrah's Blvd., 609/441-5000, www.harrahs.com) is removed from much of downtown's casino bustle. I grew up visiting Harrah's, playing Pac-Man in the arcade while my grandmother hit the slots. Though Grandmom had since moved on to Showboat, Harrah's has continued appealing to me. Maybe it's nostalgia, but it's more likely the constant upkeep employed to keep up with more centralized establishments. One of the best additions to any AC casino in recent years is Harrah's new 172,000-square-foot glass-dome-enclosed Olympic-size swimming pool surrounded by poolside cabanas, six hot tubs, and $1 million worth of greenery. The pool is for hotel guests only (21 and over, daily 7 A.M.–7 P.M.) during the day, but at night it transforms into a pulsating DJ club open to anyone (21 and over) with $10 or $20 to spare. On the casino floor is the stylish 24-hour **Xhibition Bar,** a circular lounge that's another fairly new venue.

Hunger setting in? Harrah's hosts the popular seafood restaurant **McCormick & Schmick's** (609/441-5579, Mon.–Sat. 11:30 A.M.–midnight, Sun. 11:30 A.M.–11 P.M., $15–25) and **The Taste of the Shore Food Court** (Mon. 10 A.M.–midnight, Tues.–Thurs.

9:30 A.M.–2 A.M., Fri.–Sat. 9:30 A.M.–3 A.M., Sun. 9:30 A.M.–1 A.M., $5–15), a sampling of all that's oh-so-good but bad for you, including Philly soft pretzels, hoagies, and Ben & Jerry's ice cream.

Harrah's Atlantic City sister casinos are Bally's, Caesars, and Showboat. The **Total Rewards Shuttle** runs patrons between each of the four properties.

Showboat

Since opening in the late 1980s, the Mardi Gras–themed Showboat Casino (801 Boardwalk, 609/343-4000, www.harrahs.com) had been a steady favorite with the senior slot crowd, though things changed with the resort's 2005 **House of Blues** (609/236-2583) opening. With big-name billings like B. B. King, stage acts such as *Tony n' Tina's Wedding,* and a Cajun-style House of Blues restaurant serving up slow-smoked baby back ribs ($24), chicken potpie ($15), and an awesome Sunday gospel brunch, the Boardwalk's northernmost casino suddenly got hip. An entire casino wing has been devoted to the multistory venue, nightclub, and restaurant, which also includes a souvenir shop and a slew of themed slot machines.

Showboat's other notable eateries include the **French Quarter Buffet** (Sun.–Tues. noon–9 P.M., Fri. 4–10 P.M., Sat. noon–10 P.M.), serving a Saturday-night Louisiana seafood festival ($26), and the casual **Mansion Café** (Sun.–Thurs. 7 A.M.–11 P.M., Fri.–Sat. 7 A.M.–2 A.M., $15–25), a good place for breakfast or a burger. Accommodations include the **New Orleans Tower** and the **House of Blues Studio,** which, for the loft-style bedroom, fully-stocked bar, and state-of-the-art sound system it offers, is surprisingly affordable ($360 August midweek).

The casino's Atlantic City sister properties are Bally's, Caesars, and Harrah's.

Taj Mahal

A Trump contribution to AC's skyline, the illustrious Taj (1000 Boardwalk at Virginia Ave., 609/449-1000, www.trumptaj.com) opened in 1990 with much fanfare, its onion-shaped domes and Aladdin-style lettering making it easily recognizable among the city's box-shaped buildings. The Taj is probably AC's most ornate casino, decorated in deep reds and purples accentuated in gold, with enormous chandeliers hanging in the entry halls and gambling rooms bearing names like Dragon Place and Sinbad's. Restaurants and nightclubs are also theme-based, like the extraordinary **Casbah** (800/234-5678, casbahclub.com, Fri. 10:30 P.M.–5 A.M., Sat. 10:30 P.M.6 A.M.), consistently rated the city's best dance club, and the Asian-inspired **Dynasty** (nightly from 6 P.M., $14–30), home to sushi rolls and sake martinis. The Taj features 75 regular poker tables and 14 tournament tables, second in size only to AC's Borgata.

Trump Taj Mahal is also home to the **Mark G. Etess Arena** (609/449-5150), often used for big-draw boxing matches, and **Xanadu Showroom,** where Earth, Wind, and Fire and the Monkees have performed. Additional casino highlights include AC's **Hard Rock Cafe** (1000 Boardwalk, 609/441-0007, Sun.–Thurs. 11 A.M.–midnight, Fri.–Sat. 11 A.M.–1 A.M.), the affordable all-you-can-eat **Sultan's Feast** buffet and **Casbar** bar and lounge (Fri. 9 P.M.–2 A.M., Sat. 9 P.M.–4 A.M.), located downstairs from the Casbah nightclub.

Resorts

Atlantic City's first-ever casino, the art deco Resorts (1133 Boardwalk, 800/336-6378, www .resortsac.com) debuted in 1976 in the renovated and restructured Chalfonte-Haddon Hall Hotel (a Quaker-owned hotel that once banned alcohol sales) and has been plodding along since. The casino is a sister property to AC's Hilton Casino, both owned by Colony Capital, whose additional properties include Las Vegas's Hilton Casino and Bally's Casino in Tunica, Mississippi. Resorts hosts more than 2,500 slot machines and 80 table games and features over 100,000 square feet of casino space as well as a 388-room, 27-story recently constructed hotel tower called **Rendezvous.** It can be easy to forget Resorts' long history with Atlantic City; that is, until

Resorts, Atlantic City's oldest casino

© LAURA KINIRY

you step outside its Boardwalk entry. Here, at the **Entrance to the Stars,** are the cemented signatures and handprints of famed comedians and musicians, most—like Steven Martin, Lou Rawls, and Barry Manilow—dating back to the late 1970s and early 1980s, when Atlantic City was still priming to surpass Vegas as the number 1 casino resort.

Resorts hosts a nice range of restaurants, including the upscale Italian **Capriccio,** a more casual **Gallagher's Burger Bar** (Thurs.–Sun.) and an all-you-can-eat buffet. The **Boogie Nights** nightclub, open Fridays and Saturdays, plays '70s and '80s classics (from the casino's heyday) amid bellbottom outfits and dancing roller girls. Clubbers can sip on Donny Almonds before getting groovy under spinning disco balls. Entertainers such as Tom Jones, Jerry Seinfeld, and Chris Isaak perform at the casino's 1,350-seat **Super Star Theatre** year-round.

Bally's Atlantic City

Built on the site of the historic Marlborough Blenheim Hotel, Bally's (1900 Pacific Ave.,

609/340-2000, www.harrahs.com) is a three-part casino complex made up of the original casino building, the nearby **Claridge Casino,** and the campy **Wild West Casino,** opened in 1997. The resort is expected to change names to either the Horseshoe or the Rio, although no exact timeline has been established. Due in part to the diversity of its casino floors, Bally's tends to attract a mixed-age crowd.

Bally's highlight is its Wild West Casino, a kitschy, colorful, Western-themed space decorated with steam train murals, Wells Fargo wagons, and a gold digger's wishing well. Off the main casino floor is the **Mountain Bar,** a 24-hour watering hole with a 90-foot-long bar, faux cacti, and a tiny train that circles the seating area. Live acts perform nightly throughout summer. Located upstairs, the **Virginia City Buffet** (Sun.–Thurs. 11 A.M.–9 P.M., Fri. 11 A.M.–10 P.M., Sat. 11 A.M.–11 P.M., $15–25) is a popular dining venue with older crowds.

During summer months the Wild West Casino gets second billing to Bally's **Bikini Beach Bar** (609/340-2909), arguably the best of AC's remaining beachfront venues. Umbrellaed tables, palm trees, and private gazebos leave plenty of space for yellow-bikini-clad cocktail servers to deliver drinks and Philadelphia meatheads to ogle without obstruction. DJs spin most weekday nights, and bands perform on weekends.

The resort's older Claridge wing (once a favorite of Frank Sinatra) is home to the **Blue Martini Bar,** with a menu of more than 100 martinis and a built-in frosted ice rail to keep drinks cool.

Caesars

Caesars (2100 Pacific Ave., 800/443-0104, www.caesars.com) opened in 1979 as Atlantic City's second casino, and remains one of its best known. The resort has recently undergone massive renovations, including a new facelift and the construction and opening of its upscale Pier Shops at Caesars on the historic Million Dollar Pier, across the Boardwalk from the main casino. Caesars is known for its vast slot machine selection; with more than 3,400

it's one of the city's largest. Its Roman Empire motif extends throughout the resort: Slot machines bear names like Cleopatra's Garden, the Centurion Tower provides overnight stays, and cover bands jam regularly at **Toga** (daily 11 A.M.–6 A.M.)

Caesars' restaurants include the Italian **Primavera** (Sun.–Tues. 5:30–10 P.M., Fri.–Sat. 6–10 P.M., $26–48), and the **Bacchanal** (Fri.–Sat. 6–10:30 P.M., $64.95 per person) serving a fixed-price six-course Italian meal along with strolling musicians and a never-ending wine bottle served by a Royal Maid.

Caesars' sister properties include Harrah's Atlantic City and Showboat.

Trump Plaza

Renovated in 2006, Trump Plaza (Mississippi Ave. and Boardwalk, 609/441-0608, www.trumpplaza.com) is home to one of the city's few remaining beach bars, along with the kid-friendly **Rainforest Café** (609/345-5757, $10–18), accessible from the boards. The resort's central Boardwalk location makes it popular with casino hoppers who access their spots on foot. Several years ago the main floor smelled like a mix of fast food and cigarette smoke, but that's set to change with Atlantic City Casinos' smoking ban, effective October 2008. Trump Plaza's **Liquid Bar** (800/677-7787) is a worthwhile stop, as is the Italian **Evo** (609/441-0400, daily 10 A.M.–11 P.M., $17–22), a white-linen restaurant with Boardwalk seating.

Trump Plaza remains one of the city's more lackluster casinos, though this changes seasonally with the opening of the summertime **Beach Bar,** a spacious waterfront setup with umbrella tables and open-air bars. Live music includes DJs, cover bands, and a Thursday-night Battle of the Bands.

Tropicana

Located at the Boardwalk's southern end, Tropicana Casino & Resort (S. Brighton Ave. and the Boardwalk, 609/340-4000 or 800/843-8767, www.tropicana.net) is one of the walkway's better casinos, though it was almost no more: In December 2007 the New Jersey Casino Control Commission refused to renew the Trop's gambling license, but the casino remains open under trustee supervision. Built in the early 1980s, the Tropicana has done a great job of keeping up with the times. A nongambling upscale shopping and dining addition called the Quarter and consistent renovations have scored this casino a hipper, younger crowd. With more than 2,000 guest rooms, the Tropicana is also one of Atlantic City's largest hotels.

In the center of the Trop's casino floor is the **Rumba Lounge** (daily 11:30 A.M.–3 A.M.), a panoramic-view bar with plasma TVs and live entertainment on weekends. And in the **Tropicana Marketplace** there's **Firewaters** (609/344-6699, www.firewatersbar.com), a sports bar catering to beer drinkers with 50 draft selections and more than 100 bottles. The martinis aren't so bad either.

Karaoke lovers can venture over to the Quarter's zebra-print **Planet Rose** (609/344-6565) for 365-day sing-alongs of more than 10,000 songs. The nearby **Comedy Stop** (877/386-6922, www.comedystop.com, $23) hosts an all-age espresso bar along with selected family-friendly shows for those 12 and over, and adult-only comedy entertainment throughout the week. Also in the Quarter is the crimson-coated **Red Square** (609/344-9100, www.chinagrillmgt.com/redSquareNJ/main.cfm), a vodka bar and restaurant dressed with curtain-draped tables and a photo-worthy chandelier. A statue of Lenin greets patrons on their way in. Food is served Sunday–Thursday noon–11 P.M., Friday–Saturday noon–midnight.

ENTERTAINMENT

For a flashback to Atlantic City's playground days, why not take in a ballgame at **Bernie Robbins Stadium** (545 N. Albany Ave., 609/344-8873, www.acsurf.com, $8–12), formerly called the Sandcastle. Opened in 1998, the 5,900-seat ballpark is home to Minor League Baseball's Atlantic City Surf, an independent club. It's located just off Route 322/40 on the city's southwest side.

Tropicana's **IMAX Theater** (800/843-8767, www.imaxtheaterattropicana.com, $12–14) has a 3,500-square-foot screen stretching eight stories high and a 12,000-watt digital sound system. It's the only operating theater in a city once known for them, and is located in the Tropicana Quarter.

Atlantic City Cruises (800 N. New Hampshire Ave., 609/347-7600, www.atlanticcitycruises.com, $17–33 adult, $8.50–17 child) offers cruises of 1–2 hours throughout the summer months, including dolphin-watching trips, morning skyline cruises on the ocean, and weekday happy-hour tours.

Spas

It's been only recently that Atlantic City has developed a niche reputation for spas, but there are already several fine locations to choose from. The Borgata's **Spa Toccare** (609/317-7555, Sun.–Fri. 6 A.M.–8 P.M., Sat. 6 A.M.–9 P.M.) is AC's only spa to offer the new Soft Pack system, a flotation table that warms the body while simultaneously simulating weightlessness. It increases the body's absorption rate while receiving wraps like the Firm ($115), used for reducing cellulite appearance and improving skin elasticity. On Saturdays, Spa Toccare is open to registered hotel guests only. Opened in 2008, the Water Club's two-story **Immersion** (www.theborgata.com) features a 25-yard infinity-edge lap pool and 360-degree floor-to-ceiling views from its 32nd-floor location. Tropicana Quarter's apothecary spa **Bluemercury** (www.bluemercury.com) offers 15 private rooms and treatments like the Fast Blast, a 30-minute facial glycolic peel and vitamin oxygen blast ($85); and a hydrating honey–shea butter wrap followed by a essential citrus-oil massage ($130). Opened in 2008, the Elizabeth Arden **Red Door Spa** (609/441-5333) at Harrah's offers pedicure treatment zones and separate male and female "wet zones" with steam, sauna, and Jacuzzi pools, along with co-ed relaxation areas.

NIGHTLIFE

Atlantic City is one of the state's few, if not only, 24/7 destinations. A visit to the city wouldn't be complete without a little nightlife. While there's always something happening at the casinos (for a list of options see the *Casinos* section) and on beaches throughout summer, those who'd like to experience the real AC should venture inland, away from the glitzy nightclubs and the crashing waves.

Downtown

Up on the boards just north of the Tropicana is **Flames** (2641 Boardwalk, 609/344-7774, http://flamesac.com), a long and narrow space decorated in neon tube lighting and flat-screen TVs. Though Flames doubles as a surprisingly good Mediterranean restaurant, thumping techno tunes secure its clubby ambiance even early in the afternoon. Specialty drinks include the ever-popular Sex on the Beach and the Tutti Frutti, a concoction of tequila, Midori, rum, and cranberry juice.

If you're looking to disappear, the **Irish Pub** (164 St. James Pl. at Boardwalk, 609/344-9063, www.theirishpub.com, $3–7) is the place to do it. A good old-fashioned down-and-dirty sort of place just west of the Boardwalk, it offers cheap eats and drinks and very little sunlight. The pub even rents out überbasic rooms ($20 for a bed and running water) in a Victorian above the bar, and provides an all-weather smoking patio, so you *really* never have to leave.

The brainchild of hip-hop mogul (and Beyoncé hubby) Jay-Z, Atlantic City's **New York 40/40 Club** (2120 Atlantic Ave., 609/449-4040, www.the4040club.com, Mon.–Fri. 5 P.M.–4 A.M., Sat.–Sun. noon–5 A.M.) opened along downtown's outlet shopping Walk in October 2005. Part dance club, part sports bar, part lounge and restaurant, the multilevel space manages to mix athletic memorabilia with subdued sleekness and pull it off well. The club has four VIP rooms and more than 30 TVs.

EVENTS

Get your motor running for February's annual **Antique and Classic Car Auction & Flea Market** (Atlantic City Convention Center, 800/227-3868, www.acclassiccars.com/events .html, $20), a four-day auto extravaganza. Hundreds of vintage vehicles are on display, along with hot rods, specialty cars, and an on-site auto parts swap meet. There's a side antique show of jewelry, furniture, and collectibles for anyone just along for the ride.

Some consider it to be the world's toughest swim race, which is probably why it keeps getting canceled. When weather and ocean conditions are right, several dozen men and women take to the waters for August's **Around the Island Marathon Swim** (www .acswim.org), a 22.5-mile race around Absecon Island in the Atlantic Ocean and the back bay. The event takes 7–9 hours on average to complete. Can't afford the time? Uh-huh. Why not cheer on your would-be competitors from outside Harrah's Casino, at the foot of the Brigantine Bridge?

Twice-annual **Atlantique City** (www .atlantiquecity.com) billed as "the largest indoor art, antique, and collectibles fair in the world," is one of the best in the country, a collection of books, bottle openers, clocks, cereal boxes—even coin-operated fortune-telling machines—and everything's for sale. The festival takes place in March and October at Atlantic City's Convention Hall.

SHOPPING

Worthwhile shops are a recent addition to Atlantic City's portfolio, but the city has since been wasting no time establishing its reputation as a retail destination. While most casinos have dedicated commercial space, their selection—most notably in the older casinos—is often overpriced, not to mention tacky. Things are beginning to change, but for now AC's best retail is away from the slots downtown, in the Tropicana Quarter, and along the Pier.

The Quarter

Tropicana's Cuban-inspired Quarter (Brighton and Boardwalk, 800/843-8767, www.tropicana .net/thequarter) is a multilevel shopping, dining, and entertainment plaza filled with planted palms and rounded street lamps, and sporting a painted sky ceiling that makes it feel as though you're strolling along a Havana Street. There's no need to step inside a casino to explore this Cuban paradise—while it's part of the Tropicana complex, it's completely self-contained. Restaurants and bars center around Fiesta Plaza, the integral fountain and square, and at night their occupants spill onto the circular balconies as if the party were truly spreading outdoors.

The Quarter is home to an Imax theater, Atlantic City's only movie theater, along with retail shops such as Chico's and Brooks Brothers. The specialty shopping is some of the city's best, with stores like **The Spy Store** (609/348-1500), stocking body recorders and surveillance cameras; **Klassic Kollectables** (609/344-1191), home to autographed photos and Betty Boop souvenirs; the aptly named **Hat Emporium** (609/348-1777); and **Bluemercury Apothecary** (609/347-7778), where you can pick up bottles of Kiehl's Ultimate Thickening Shampoo and Trish McEvoy moisturizer.

The Walk

Just a few steps away from Atlantic City's train and bus depot and convention center is a neon-lit open-air bargain shopper's paradise. Stretching along Michigan Avenue between Baltic and Artic Avenues, the Walk (609/343-0081, www.acoutlets.com, Mon.–Sat. 10 A.M.–9 P.M., Sun. 10 A.M.–8 P.M.) is home to factory and outlet stores such as Guess, Nike, Converse, Brooks Brothers, and Banana Republic, interspersed with eateries like Stewart's Root Beer to help keep energy levels up.

The Pier

Though you may have fond memories of the faux ocean liner once standing in its place, **The Pier Shops at Caesars** (1 Atlantic Ocean, 609/345-3100, www.thepiershopsat caesars.com, Mon.–Thurs. 11 A.M.–10 P.M., Fri. 11 A.M.–11 P.M., Sat. 10 A.M.–11 P.M., Sun. 10 A.M.–9 P.M.) is a different beast entirely: more upscale, more diverse, and much more refined. This multilevel shopping plaza is home to such high-class stores as Apple, Betsey

Johnson, Burberry, and Gucci, along with area favorites Steven Madden and James' Salt Water Taffy. Restaurants include **Sonsie** (609/345-6300, www.sonsieac.com, daily 10 A.M.–closing), a Boston favorite serving dishes like strawberry-stuffed French toast ($12) and prosciutto and pepperoni calzone ($14) for breakfast and lunch, and spice-crusted yellowfin tuna ($27) for dinner; and **The Continental** (Mon.–Thurs. 11:30 A.M.–10 P.M., Fri.–Sat. 11:30 A.M.–midnight, Sun. 11 A.M.–10 P.M., $15–30), a retro populuxe eatery complete with a fire-pit lounge and menu of global tapas.

A glass skyway extending over the Boardwalk connects the Pier with Caesars casino.

ACCOMMODATIONS

With more than 15,000 guest rooms within city limits, Atlantic City has no shortage of overnight accommodations. That being said, some are far better than others. While change is on the rise, the city is first and foremost a casino resort—they want you on the floor, not in the bed—and hotels in general are not a reason to book a trip here. Still, there are some fine choices, many of which offer discounts to casino regulars and AAA members. For the best deals, call well ahead.

Though motels line the roads in and out of the city, they can be seedy. Try nearby Somers Point for affordable alternatives.

Casino Hotels

Atlantic City's casinos are required by law to include hotels, but they've long been a secondary feature to gambling. That's now changing, with many casinos building newer luxury hotel towers to attract younger crowds. These same casinos have held onto their older towers, so it's important to specify your room type and tower preference when making reservations.

While fluctuating room rates are common in every shore town, with prices highest on weekends and July–August, Atlantic City's hotel rooms can run anywhere from $99 to $500 per night, depending on whether you're a frequent casino patron, when you call (rates change daily), and whether you book your room as part of a package deal. Rates below are based on midweek high season.

$150-300

Constructed in 2003, the Showboat's **New Orleans Tower** (801 Boardwalk, 800/621-0200, www.harrahs.com, $189–239) is the best lodging choice for those planning trips to the Boardwalk's northern attractions, including the Atlantic City Historical Museum and the Steel Pier. Many rooms offer excellent ocean views, along with plush headboards and plasma TVs. For central Boardwalk attractions, including Boardwalk Hall, book a **deluxe room at Bally's** (1900 Pacific Ave., 800/277-5990, www.harrahs.com, $149–179). Amenities include ample closet space and dark wood furnishings.

Another fairly recent addition to AC's skyline is Tropicana's **Havana Tower** (S. Brighton Ave. and Boardwalk, 800/345-8767, www.tropicana.net/thequarter, $149–169), perched above shopping and dining mecca the Quarter. Rooms are clean but basic; they're a good choice for a one-stop shopping stay.

Resorts may be Atlantic City's first casino, but its 27-story art deco–style **Rendezvous Tower** (Resorts, 1113 Boardwalk, 800/336-6378, www.resortsac.com, $145–175) is still in its early years. Rooms are some of the city's largest, and include oversized bathrooms and double-sized showers. The tower also features 58 suites complete with panoramic ocean views. It's a popular place, so book early.

Currently Atlantic City's tallest structure, Harrah's new 44-story **Waterfront Tower** (777 Harrah's Blvd., 609/441-5000, www.harrahs.com, $199–259) features 500-square-foot rooms, each with 42-inch flat-screen TVs, separate seating areas, dark wood furnishings, and a granite and tile spa shower. The tower also hosts 112 suites complete with fireplaces and in-room theaters. Harrah's more affordable Marina Tower isn't so bad either, offering chic luxury rooms ($169–229) with hardwood floors and urban decor. And here's the best part: Overnight stays come with use of the resort's brand-new dome-enclosed Olympic-size pool.

$300-450

As Atlantic City's newest casino, it's hard to go wrong with the bayside **Borgata** (1 Borgata Way, 866/692-6742, www.theborgata.com, $279–299). Modern rooms are bathed in neutral colors and host floor-to-ceiling windows, and many offer spectacular views of the Boardwalk's neon skyline. Guests have access to an indoor pool and wet bar, along with ample shopping, eats, and gambling down below. Although prices may skyrocket over summer weekends, keep in mind that prices are for the room and not the number of occupants.

Even better than the casino accommodations is Borgata's new **Water Club** (1 Renaissance Way, 800/800-8817, www.thewaterclubhotel.com, $329–379), a 43-story boutique hotel opened in summer 2008. Each of the 800 rooms offers water views, along with 400-thread-count sheets, wireless Internet, and LCD TVs. But that's just the beginning. Guests also have access to five heated pools, a sunroom lobby lounge, and an on-site spa.

Noncasino Hotels

You'll find plenty of noncasino hotels catering to Atlantic City visitors, but only a few real standouts (including a brand-new hotel that'll spoil you rotten). About a half-hour's drive south, Ocean City offers several bed-and-breakfast options. There's also a good B&B in Ventnor, the next town south from Atlantic City.

$100-300

If you don't mind driving, the **Hampton Inn Atlantic City Bayside** (7079 Black Horse Pk. and Rte. 40, West Atlantic City, 609/484-1900, $95–140), located a few miles west of AC, is a clean, affordable overnight option with its own bayside beach. The hotel offers complimentary breakfast daily and wireless Internet throughout.

Attached to AC's Convention Center, beside the train station and within easy walking distance of the city's outlet shopping, is the 15-story **Sheraton Atlantic City** (2 Miss America Way, 609/344-3535, www.sheraton.com/atlanticcity, $99–183 s, $189–329 d), a lush hotel with art deco–designed rooms and comfy beds, and some excellent skyline views. In addition to a gift shop, swimming pool, and the city's only brewery-restaurant, the Sheraton hosts the largest collection of Miss America memorabilia in existence, including past contestants' evening gowns and shoes, in its lobby.

$300-450

Seems like stand-alone luxe lodgings in AC went the way of its America's Playground image, until ❮ **The Chelsea** (111 S. Chelsea Ave., thechelsea-ac.com) opened in 2008. The 20-story hotel, an adaptive refurbishment of both the Holiday Inn Atlantic City and the adjacent Howard Johnson's Hotel, is the city's first noncasino Boardwalk hotel opened since the 1960s. With its two Stephen Starr restaurants, a saltwater-inspired spa, fireplace lounges, and an entirely full-service beach, the Chelsea oozes glamour. Just sip a mojito in one of its bars, or book a poolside cabana, and you'll see. A flat-screen TV, minibar, bathrobes and bath amenities, and Wi-Fi are customary in every room, and many offer water views. But luxury doesn't come cheap: Rooms run $299–499 August midweek, and if you really want to splurge there's the ultimate penthouse suite ($3,500), complete with sweeping ocean views, a master bedroom, and a sunroom with floor-to-ceiling windows. Did I mention the kitchen, balcony, and 42-inch flat-screen TV?

FOOD
Downtown

Atlantic City's most cherished dining establishments exist outside the casinos and off the boards, spread through downtown.

Located in the heart of the city's Ducktown Italian district is **Angelo's Fairmount Tavern** (2300 Fairmount Ave., 609/344-2439, www.angelosfairmounttavern.com, lunch Mon.–Fri. 11:30 A.M.–3 P.M., dinner Mon.–Fri. 5–11 P.M., Sat.–Sun. 4:30–11 P.M.), about as far from the bright lights and big buildings defining present-day AC as you can get. A classic Italian family-owned eatery opened in 1935, Angelo's serves heaping portions of old favorites like

stuffed rigatoni ($12.95) and linguine and crab ($19.75), accompanied by bread and large house salads. The loud, bustling restaurant is separated from a cozy upfront bar by a door. Decor includes framed baseball photos and an autographed Sinatra shot.

Another old-school haunt, known for its 24-hour bar and standard pizzas, **Tony's Baltimore Grill** (2800 Atlantic Ave., 609/345-5766, www.baltimoregrill.com, $4–12) also serves an unbelievably affordable selection of seafood, sandwich, and pasta dishes. Not much has changed in the 40-plus years this place has been in business; not even the jukeboxes, which still play 45s.

You won't find a better sandwich shop than **White House Sub Shop** (2301 Arctic Ave., 609/345-1564, Mon.–Thurs. 10 A.M.–9:30 P.M., Fri.–Sat. 10 A.M.–10:30 P.M., Sun. 11 A.M.–9 P.M., $6–11). In business since 1946, this Atlantic City gem hosts out-the-door lines of folks waiting to get their hands on a Philly cheese steak or Italian sausage sub almost daily. Sinatra had become such a fan it's rumored he had their sandwiches flown to him while performing in Vegas. The towel Frank used in his last AC performance hangs sealed on the wall.

For more than a century, family-owned ❮ **Dock's Oyster House** (2405 Atlantic Ave., 609/345-0092, www.docksoysterhouse.com, Sun.–Thurs. 5–10 P.M., Fri.–Sat. 5–11 P.M., $24–53) has been delivering consistently appetizing seafood dishes. The raw bar is especially popular. A gracious staff and the best margaritas in town are both reasons to visit **Los Amigos** (1926 Atlantic Ave., 609/344-2293, www.losamigosrest.com, Mon.–Sat. 11:30 A.M.–1 A.M., Sun. 11:30 A.M.–10 P.M., 7–12), although the fish tacos ($10.95) aren't so bad either.

Attached to the Sheraton Hotel within walking distance of the train station is **Tun Tavern Brewery & Restaurant** (2 Miss America Way, 609/347-7800, www.tuntavern.com, Sun.–Tues. 11:30 A.M.–midnight, Wed.–Sat. 11:30 A.M.–2 A.M.) Atlantic City's first and only restaurant–brew pub. Cuisine includes steak, seafood, and signature entrées like chicken and shrimp marsala ($21.99), but the real highlight here is the drinks. Try the bitter Bullies Brown Ale or the aptly named Leatherneck Stout, or for something unusual, request a made-to-order fruit beer. Located in the city's quieter Gardener's Basin, the lax **Back Bay Ale House** (800 N. New Hampshire Ave., 609/449-0006, www.backbayalehouse.com, daily 11 A.M.–9:30 P.M. summer, $8–26) serves favored American eats like the eight-ounce Cheese Burger in Paradise ($7.99) along with a selection of beers and wines. Request a table on the second-story enclosed deck for superb sunset views.

The Quarter

Atlantic City's newer shopping centers also feature some of the city's best upscale dining experiences. Tropicana's Quarter is home to several, including restaurant and rum bar **Cuba Libre** (The Quarter, 609/348-6700, www.cubalibrerestaurant.com, daily 11:30 A.M.–11 P.M., $18.50–32). With its dimmed lights, palm trees, balcony terrace, and grand staircase, this place feels more like it belongs in the Caribbean than on the Jersey coast—just what its designers were hoping for. Classy Cuban eats include *ropa vieja,* a shredded beef brisket stew, and seviche on toasted flatbread. Come evening, the restaurant morphs into a salsa dance club (Fri.–Sat. until 4 A.M.), spilling out onto the Quarter's square.

Originating in New York City, **Carmines** (The Quarter, 609/572-9300, www.carminesnyc.com, Sun.–Thurs. 11:30 A.M.–midnight, Fri.–Sat. 11:30 A.M.–1 A.M., $19–40) serves southern Italian specialties like rigatoni ($26.50) and manicotti ($27), along with vegetable and sausage sides, in family-sized portions made to share. The restaurant's classic decor includes framed celebrity shots and photos of former Miss America beauty queens. Winter hours vary; call ahead.

Semichain **Ri Ra** (The Quarter, 609/348-8600, www.rira.com, daily 11 A.M.–closing, $10–20) is as Irish as they come. Guests dine on beef 'n' Guinness stew ($12) and shepherd's pie ($12) in a darkened interior decked with salvaged Irish goods. Even the staff is Irish. The place morphs into a nightclub Thursday–Saturday 11 P.M.–3 A.M., with live bands and dance.

INFORMATION AND SERVICES

Visit the **Atlantic City Convention & Visitors Authority** website (www.atlanticcitynj.com) or call their hotline (888/228-4748) for up-to-date details on what's happening in and around the city. Once in town, the **Boardwalk Information Center** (Boardwalk Hall, Boardwalk and Mississippi Ave., daily 9:30 A.M.–5:30 P.M. year-round) has reps on hand to answer questions, and there's a fully stocked display of free hotel, restaurant, and activity flyers. You can also stop by the **Atlantic City Expressway Visitor Welcome Center** (Atlantic City Expressway Mile Marker 3.5, daily 9 A.M.–5 P.M. year-round) for information on the drive into AC.

GETTING THERE AND AROUND

The **Atlantic City Expressway** is the most direct and quickest route (sans weekend traffic) to AC from both South Jersey and Philadelphia. From Philly's Walt Whitman or Ben Franklin Bridge, exit onto I-295 south to Route 42, which leads directly to the Expressway. It's about an hour's drive from beginning to end, but bring lots of cash for tolls. A Pennsylvania alternative is the Commodore Barry Bridge (south of Philadelphia International Airport) to Route 322, which eventually joins the Black Horse Pike (Route 42) and becomes Albany Boulevard just outside Atlantic City. The road leads directly into the city.

For those traveling the **Garden State Parkway** from New York City and North Jersey, take Exits 40 or 38; if you're coming north from Cape May, take Exits 36 or 38.

NJ Transit trains run from the Philadelphia Amtrak Station and take 90 minutes one-way. A round-trip ticket costs $16. Free shuttle service is available between AC's transit terminal and the city's casinos. There's no train service from New York City, but it is supposedly in the works.

It's easy to find all-inclusive bus packages to AC from both Philadelphia and New York, as well as from numerous towns and cities throughout New Jersey. Churches, Elks lodges, synagogues—everyone seems to be running them, and you often get cash back from casinos in the form of slot credits or a meal.

Spirit Airlines (www.spiritair.com) flies daily into **Atlantic City International Airport** (609/645-7895, www.acairport.com) from cities like Las Vegas, Los Angeles, and Fort Lauderdale.

Once in the city, **Jitneys** (609/344-8642, www.jitneys.net, $2.25) are a good way to get around. These 13-passenger blue buses operate along various number- and color-coded routes throughout AC: Number 1 Pink travels back and forth along Pacific Avenue, Number 2 Blue and Number 3 Green both operate to and from the Marina and its bayside casinos, and the Number 4 Orange picks up and drops off at the Convention Center, train station, and bus terminal. Most Jitney's run 24/7 (the Number 4 Orange runs daily 7 A.M.–7 P.M.) and can be accessed from various points along Pacific Avenue (look for the color-coded signs adorning street corners one block west of the Boardwalk casinos).

Greater Atlantic City Region

Atlantic City's surrounding shore towns and mainland suburbs offer lax alternatives to their big-city neighbor. The region is home to some excellent golf courses, affordable accommodation, lively beaches, and a handful of wineries, not to mention top-notch restaurants in Margate.

BRIGANTINE

Just north of Atlantic City is the quiet island city of Brigantine (www.brigantinbeachnj.com), accessible only by Route 87, which runs along AC's bay. Although mostly residential, the entire north end of the city's nearly 10 miles remains undeveloped, protected as a wildlife habitat. The name Brigantine means "two-masted vessel," a fitting memorial to the hundreds of shipwrecks that occurred off the city's coast over the centuries.

Brigantine was home of the infamous **Brigantine Castle,** a "haunted" walk-through dark ride that stood on the former Seahorse Pier during the late 1970s and 1980s. The castle burned down in 1987 after having been closed for several years, but I can assure you, it lives on in the memories—and nightmares—of South Jerseyans everywhere.

E. B. Forsythe National Wildlife Refuge

Brigantine's E. B. Forsythe National Wildlife Refuge (Great Creek Rd., 609/652-1665, http://forsythe.fws.gov, daily dawn–dusk, $4 vehicle, $2 walk-in or bicycle, under 16 free) is a birder's paradise. Filled with salt meadows, marshlands, tall grass, and scrub, it's one of New Jersey's best places for spotting egrets, herons, geese, mallards, and other waterfowl. An eight-mile one-way dirt trail open to cars and bicycles is dotted with points of interest and includes several pullouts (the 15-mile-per-hour speed limit can be a problem for tailgaters). It also offers an interesting juxtaposing view of Atlantic City's casinos in the distance. There are several walking trails, although ticks, mosquitoes, and greenflies are problematic during summer months. The best times to visit are in May and October, when the Atlantic Flyway (a migratory bird route) is in full swing and bugs are at a minimum. Printouts describing trail points are available at the information kiosk, and restrooms are situated nearby. If the kiosk is closed, stop by park headquarters (just south of the driving loop's entrance, weekdays 8 A.M.–4 P.M.) for info and pamphlets. And don't forget your binoculars!

Other Sights

Brigantine's **Marine Mammal Stranding Center** (3625 Brigantine Blvd., 609/266-0538, www.marinemammalstrandingcenter.org, $1) cares for sea life such as dolphins, turtles, and whales injured along the Jersey coast, in the hope of rereleasing them. In operation for more than 20 years, the center is in danger of closing when its city lease expires in 2010, if local officials decide there's a more valuable use for the waterfront property. For now, guests can visit the **Sea Life Education Center** (Tues.–Sat. 10 A.M.–3 P.M. Memorial Day–Labor Day, winter hours vary) and view regional sea life in an underwater tank, along with locally found shells and marine mammal bones, and life-size replicas of marine mammals and fish.

Just down the road from Brigantine's Wildlife Refuge is the **Noyes Museum of Art** (733 Lily Lake Rd., Oceanville, 609/652-8848, www.noyesmuseum.org, Tues.–Sat. 10 A.M.–4:30 P.M., Sun. noon–5 P.M., $4 adult, under 12 free), recently celebrating 25 years. The museum is one of the southern Shore's largest and most well-respected, displaying both folk art and fine art pieces, including a collection of vintage bird decoys once belonging to founder Frank Noyes.

Beaches

Daily beach tags cost $7, $17 for the season, age 12 and under free.

ABSECON

Two miles west of Absecon Bay, Absecon is a mainland community close enough to both Atlantic City and its shore towns directly south to be a good overnight alternative. The area features a range of lodging choices from chain hotels to campgrounds.

Storybook Land

Situated along Route 42 (Black Horse Pike) west of Atlantic City, Storybook Land (6415 Black Horse Pike, Cardiff, 609/641-7847 or 609/646-0103, ext. 5, www.storybookland.com, $19.95) has been a favorite fairy-tale theme park for more than 50 years. Every kid (and adult) who's driven past the roadside castle and its property walls longs to get a glimpse inside. The park has expanded over the years but remains as charming as its beginnings. You can still visit the home of the Three Bears, tumble down Jack and Jill's slide, and tour Alice in Wonderland's Day-Glo cave, which opens out to a life-size maze of playing cards; and mechanical rides include a carousel, the Happy Dragon airlift ride, and Bubbles the roller coaster. It's a fun place to visit in summer, but it's breathtaking (literally) in winter, when hundreds of thousands of colored lights are displayed. A visit during the holiday season makes a great date or family outing—adults will enjoy the scenery as much as kids, a new generation that'll hopefully keep the park up and running for another half century.

Storybook Land's hours vary depending on the season, but are normally weekends 11:30 A.M.–5:30 P.M. in late March and April, daily 11:30 A.M.–5:30 P.M. in summer, and daily 2–9 P.M. during winter.

WINERIES

The Jersey Shore's climate produces long growing seasons and nutrient-rich soil ideal for vineyards. For this reason several wineries have popped up along the state's southern coast over the last couple of centuries.

Renault Winery

My, how you've grown, Renault Winery (72 N. Bremen Ave., Egg Harbor City, 609/965-2111, www.renaultwinery.com). Once a fairly modest establishment, this 1864 winery—one of oldest continuously operating wineries in the country—is now a massive resort, home to a championship golf course and the imposing Tuscany House Hotel and Restaurant. The winery and its restaurant remain my favorites, connected to one another by a lakeside European-style courtyard. Winery tours (609/965-2111) begin in the Fountain Room and continue onto the property's antique-glass museum, hospitality room, and later, the grape pressing room before concluding with wine tastings. If you're planning to visit over a weekend, don't miss the

Renault Gourmet Restaurant's Sunday brunch (10 A.M.–2 P.M., $19.95), a feast of decadent foods and mimosas set in a dimly lit castle-like space. Winery tours run approximately ever 20 minutes, beginning daily at 10 A.M., with evening hours on Friday and Saturday. Renault Gourmet Restaurant is open Friday 5–8 P.M., Saturday 5–9 P.M., and Sunday 10 A.M.–2 P.M. and 4:30–7 P.M.

Tomasello Winery

Founded in 1933, Tomasello Winery (225 White Horse Pike, Hammonton, 888/666-9463, www.tomasellowinery.com, Mon.–Wed. 9 A.M.–6 P.M., Thurs.–Sat. 9 A.M.–8 P.M., Sun. 11 A.M.–6 P.M.) is the largest of the state's more than 30 wineries, a family-run establishment specializing in red raspberry and blackberry dessert wines, and premium wines such as cabernet sauvignon and pinot noir. The winery has a free tasting room and a vintner's room where annual galas are held (check the website for a schedule).

Balic Winery

Chateau Balic (6623 Rte. 40, May's Landing, 609/625-2166, www.balicwinery.com) opened in the 1960s and today features more than 27 award-winning wines, including an American Cream Red and a pomegranate wine. A tasting room is open to the public Monday–Saturday 9 A.M.–8 P.M. and Sunday 11 A.M.–7 P.M.

GOLF

Golfing is a popular regional activity, and the greater Atlantic City area hosts several good courses. These are the best.

Harbor Pines Golf Club's (500 St. Andrews Dr., Egg Harbor Township, 609/927-0006, www.harborpines.com, $65–115 daily) 18-hole course is known for its wide fairways and wooded seclusion. On-site classes are offered for anyone wanting to improve their game (609/927-0006, ext. 10).

Fifteen minutes from Atlantic City, **Blue Heron Pines Golf Club** (W. Country Club Dr., Cologne, 609/965-1800, www.blueheronpines.com, $69–99) is an 18-hole championship golf course awarded a 4.5-star rating by *Golf Digest* magazine.

Part of the exquisite 670-acre Seaview Marriott Resort just off Route 9 is **Seaview Marriott Golf Club** (410 S. New York Rd., Galloway, 609/652-1800, www.seaviewgolf.com), 36 holes divided between two courses, each in play since the early 20th century. The annual Shop Rite LPGA Classic takes place on the renowned Bay Course, and a gorgeous 297-room luxury hotel adorns the property. Rates run $29–129 depending on the time of day, week, and year.

VENTNOR, MARGATE, AND LONGPORT

Just south of Atlantic City are the towns of Ventnor, Margate, and Longport, three shore communities making up the remainder of Absecon Island and referred to locally as "Downbeach." Driving through them, you get a feel for what Atlantic City must've been like when it was "America's Playground," before its fall from grace and the advent of the casinos. Homes are grand and stately, and many have been around since the early 20th century. The three towns are much (*much*) more residential than their northern neighbor, filled with pleasant shops, ice cream parlors, greenery, and front yards, along with some excellent restaurants. The best attraction, however, stands tall in Margate: With her long trunk and white tusks you can't miss her. Her name's Lucy, and believe me, she's something worth seeing.

◖ Lucy the Elephant

No, you're not seeing things. That *is* a 65-foot-tall wooden elephant (9200 Atlantic Ave., Margate, 609/823-6473, www.lucytheelephant.org, $6 adult, $3 child) standing along Margate's shore. She goes by the name of Lucy (though with those tusks she's really a he), and she was one of three elephant structures built in the late 1800s in New Jersey and New York. Lucy came about in 1881 as a way of luring prospective buyers to Absecon Island, and has since withstood disastrous ocean winds, encroaching development, and time. Now a historic landmark, Lucy has survived her two wooden siblings by more than a century. Cape May County's zoomorphic structure burned down in 1896, while New York's Coney Island tore down their elephant, which operated as a hotel, in 1900. Lucy has been used as a tavern and private residence, and today as a multistory museum. Things haven't always been easy for Lucy: She's faced extinction numerous times, and was once pulled along Margate's streets for seven hours to settle at her current home. In 2006 the howdah on her back was struck by lightening, causing damage that cost $145,000 to repair. But at nearly 130 years old, Lucy is looking better than ever, with bright painted toenails and a fresh coat of paint. She's the most frequented nongaming attraction in the Atlantic City area—be sure to pay her a visit.

Lucy's open for tours Monday–Saturday 10 A.M.–8 P.M. and Sunday 10 A.M.–5 P.M. during summer. Call ahead for off-season hours.

For Lucy bobbleheads, books, DVDs, and miniatures, stop by the **Lucy Souvenir Cart** (Artic and Michigan Aves., Mon.–Sat. noon–8 P.M., Sun. 11 A.M.–5 P.M. summer, Sat.–Sun. 11 A.M.–5 P.M. off-season) along the Walk in Atlantic City.

Beaches

Beach tags for Ventnor and Margate each cost $15 for the season, free for those age 12 and under. Longport sells season tags for $30 and weekly tags for $10 ($5 senior), with age 12 and under free. Tags cannot be interchanged among the three towns. Margate has a public restroom at Huntington Avenue and the beach.

Sports and Recreation

Go old-school putt-putt style at the seasonal **Margate Miniature Golf** (211 N. Jefferson Ave., 609/822-0660). Rent clunky cruisers ($10 for a half day) and four-wheel surreys ($20 per hour) at Ventnor's **AAAA Bike Shop** (5300 Ventnor Ave., 609/487-0808, www.aaaabike shop.com), in business for over 25 years. Bicycling is allowed on Ventnor's boardwalk Sunday–Thursday 6 A.M.–noon and 5–7 P.M.,

and on Atlantic City's connecting Boardwalk daily 6 A.M.–10 A.M.

Ventnor's noncommercial boardwalk attaches to the south end of Atlantic City's, extending the famous "B" by nearly two miles. There's also a long public fishing pier.

Accommodations

With only 10 rooms, Ventnor's **Carisbrooke Inn Bed and Breakfast** (105 S. Little Rock Ave., 609/822-6392, www.carisbrookeinn .com, $171–246) offers a nice alternative to Atlantic City's bustling hotels. Each individually styled room has its own private bath, along with a flat-panel TV, DVD player (and access to the inn's DVD library), central air, and wireless Internet. Guests are treated to complimentary wine and refreshments each evening, served on the ocean-view deck during summer months and fireside in winter. The inn stands on the original spot of Ventnor's first hotel.

Food

For breakfast don't miss Ventnor's colorful **Ma France Creperie** (5213 Ventnor Ave., 609/399-9955, Mon.–Sat. 8 A.M.–9 P.M., Sun. 8 A.M.–3 P.M., $5–15), a traditional French crepe restaurant serving sweet and savory crepes along with a selection of salads and quiche.

Tomatoes (9300 Amherst Ave., Margate, 609/822-7535, www.tomatoesmargate.com, Sun.–Thurs. 5–10 P.M., Fri.–Sat. 5–11 P.M., $31–49) is known for its upscale Asian-influenced eats and sharp decor. While the sushi bar is impressive, it doesn't top this BYO's glass-enclosed climate-controlled wine cellar stocked with thousands of vintages.

Considered one of Margate's great restaurants, ◖ **Steve & Cookie's by the Bay** (9700 Amherst Ave., 609/823-1163, www.steveand cookies.com, Sun.–Thurs. 5–10 P.M., Fri.–Sat. 5–11 P.M., $17–49) is both classy and consistent, serving seafood-heavy New American dishes in a waterside locale offering fantastic over-the-inlet sunset views. Highlights include an oyster bar and a to-die-for chocolate peanut-butter pie ($7.50).

Getting There

To reach Ventnor take Garden State Parkway Exits 38 or 36 (southbound) or Exits 29 or 36 (northbound). For Margate and Longport use the Parkway's Exit 36. There's a toll to reach Margate from the mainland. No tolls exist between Atlantic City and Longport.

SMITHVILLE

Things weren't looking too good for Smithville a couple of decades ago. The town had changed ownership numerous times since its late-18th-century beginnings, and many of its buildings had fallen into disrepair. You wouldn't know that by visiting Smithville now, especially when stopping by its Village Greene (1 N. New York Rd. at Rte. 9, 609/652-7777, www.smithvillenj .com), a restored shopping village made up of historic structures brought together from throughout South Jersey, interspersed with brick lanes and centered around a small lake and boardwalk. Antiques, Christmas ornaments, Irish flags, and framed celebrity photos are all for sale here, and attractions include an arcade shooting gallery, a miniature train, and paddleboat rentals (609/748-6160). In addition, the Greene is home to several dining options (including a historic inn), a bed-and-breakfast that suites the surrounding theme, and a number of festivals and events throughout the year. Smithville has become a great day-trip and family destination. Kids will especially love the geese and ducks frequently backing up traffic on area roadways.

Shopping

With more than 60 shops and restaurants, you'll find plenty to do in Smithville. Notable stores include **Ireland and Old Lace** (609/404-0477, www.irelandandoldlace .com), home to cable-knit sweaters and gold Claddagh rings; UK novelty shop **The British Connection** (609/404-4444); a smattering of craft and antique shops such as **Country Folk** (609/652-6161) and **Crafting Cellar** (609/404-3333); specialty soap purveyor **Little Egg Harbor Soap** (609/652-9300, www .LittleEggHarborSoap.com); and pooch-perfect **PawDazzle Pet Boutique** (609/748-7110). Shops are open daily year-round, with summer

© LAURA KINIRY

Smithville, along Route 9

hours Monday–Wednesday 10 A.M.–6 P.M., Thursday–Saturday 10 A.M.–8 P.M., and Sunday 11 A.M.–6 P.M.

Accommodations

It's easy to turn a trip to Smithville into a relaxing shopping weekend, especially if spending the night at the Village Greene's **Colonial Inn Bed & Breakfast** (615 E. Moss Rd., 609/748-8999, www.colonialinnsmithville.com, $149–199), situated next to the main parking lot. The inn offers eight traditionally styled guest rooms, all with private baths and bubble tubs, outdoor decks, and a TV and DVD player, and some offer panoramic views of the property's Lake Meone. Shops and restaurants are literally right outside your door, and a coffee shop is housed on-site. Overnight stays come with complimentary breakfast.

Food

A Smithville highlight is the **Smithville Inn** (Rte. 9 and Moss Mill Rd., 609/652-7777, www.smithvilleinn.com, Mon.–Thurs. 11:30 A.M.–9 P.M., Fri.–Sat. 11:30 A.M.–9:30 P.M., Sun. 10 A.M.–8 P.M., $18–29), a historic 1787 property with a patio room overlooking Lake Meone. It's one of the Greene's few original structures, and both decor and cuisine are traditional, with multiple fireplaces, exposed wood beams, and dishes like flaky-crust chicken potpie and Chesapeake crab cakes.

For those in the market for more casual fare, visit **Fred & Ethel's Lantern Light Tavern** (609/652-0544, Mon.–Thurs. 11:30 A.M.–2 A.M., Fri.–Sat. 11:30 A.M.–3 A.M., Sun. 11:30 A.M.–midnight, $9–18), also located in the village. This family-friendly place—named for Smithville's original founders, Fred and Ethel Noyes—hosts a popular weekday happy hour and serves a standard menu of American burgers, soups, and platters. Live music plays most weekends.

The Cape

The Jersey Shore's southernmost beach towns are some of its best. Sure, I'm biased, but with places like family-friendly Ocean City, wildlife-friendly Stone Harbor, and stunning Cape May, it's hard to go wrong. It seems like there's a place for everyone along New Jersey's southern shore, including naturalists, adrenaline junkies, romantics, and historians. Ocean City and Wildwood offer two of the state's best boardwalks, and Cape May features some of New Jersey's finest eats. One of New Jersey's best drives is along the unofficial Ocean Drive, a stretch of road connecting Ocean City straight through to Cape May, passing through every shore town along the way. Bridges connect the islands, and each has a $1 toll payable in one direction.

◖ OCEAN CITY

Founded by Methodist ministers as a 19th-century religious summer retreat, Ocean City remains an all-around family favorite. In addition to an abundance of summer rentals, the city hosts wonderful eateries, dozens of activities (including the crowing of Miss New Jersey *and* Miss Crustacean), and one of the Shore's best all-around boardwalks. As Ocean City's biggest draw, the 2.5-mile walkway attracts quite a crowd, who come for its amusements, arcade games, shops, and old-school miniature golf courses. The boardwalk hasn't changed much in the 30-some years I've been frequenting it. It's been widened and rebuilt in parts, but the Music Pier remains, as do the historic movie theaters, Mac & Mancos pizza stands, and Kohrs Bros. ice cream windows.

Ocean City has long had a problem with beach erosion—sand seems to wash south toward Wildwood with every storm. The city spends millions (your beach tag dollars at work) to replenish the beaches, only to watch them disappear again…and again.

Ocean City's Spanish-style downtown center

stretches along Asbury Avenue around Ninth Street, and it includes several interesting shops and restaurants. On the city's northern tip is the Garden District, a residential neighborhood that more resembles towns like Margate and Ventnor than Sea Isle and Avalon to the south. Corsen's Inlet lies along Ocean Drive toward Ocean City's southern end. En route to Strathmere and Sea Isle, the park offers a quiet reprieve from the typical Shore action.

Boardwalk

If I were to offer New Jersey an award for best boardwalk, I'd give it to Ocean City. This 2.5-mile walkway has just the right mix: not too crazy, not too calm, with long empty stretches ideal for walkers and runners, and a central hub that's built up on one side with shops, hotels, snack stands, and attractions, without blocking ocean views. The historic Music Pier is the only true structure on the boardwalk's western side, and it's lovely—a Spanish-style architectural masterpiece that juts out into the ocean, adding to the walkway's scenic allure. Games of chance don't exist (this is a religious town), but the amusement rides, shooting galleries, miniature golf courses, and multitude of fried-food options can keep you busy for hours. Some of my favorite boardwalk shops include **Air Circus** (1114 Boardwalk, 609/399-9343), which carries an awesome selection of colorful kites; the pricey but fun to browse **Only Yesterday** (1108 Boardwalk, 609/398-2869) collectibles store; **Islander** (922 Boardwalk, 609/398-3069), stocking one of the walkway's most varied clothing selections; and **7th Street Surf Shop** (654 Boardwalk, 609/391-1700, http://7thstreetsurfshop.com), offering daily summer surf lessons at 8 A.M. and 10:30 A.M. on the Seventh Street Beach ($35 per person). For one of the best boardwalk experiences, get up early and rent a beach cruiser to ride the boards before 11 A.M., breaking at one of the walkway's eateries for breakfast. Info on bicycle rentals is available under *Sports and Recreation.*

Other Sights

The **Discovery Seashell Museum** (2717 Asbury Ave., 609/398-2316, www.shellmuseum .com, Mon.–Sat. 10 A.M.–8 P.M., Sun. noon–6 P.M. Apr.–Oct., free) is a fun place to browse any time, but it's especially so on a

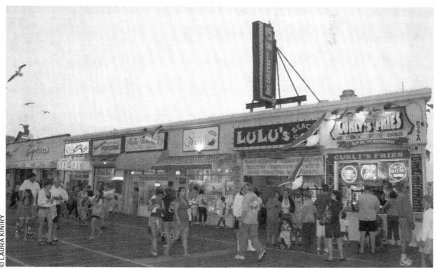

© LAURA KINIRY

Ocean City's boardwalk at dusk

© LAURA KINIRY

giant Ferris wheel, Gillian's Wonderland Pier, Ocean City

drizzly summer day. More of a store than a museum, there are hundreds of thousands of shells from around the globe here, along with giant coral and shark's teeth. Seashell-decorated change purses, shell necklaces, and carved-shell rings make great souvenirs.

Located in the city's large Cultural Arts Center alongside an aquatic and fitness center and a public library is the **Ocean City Historical Museum** (1735 Simpson Ave., 609/399-1801, www.ocnjmuseum.org, Mon.–Fri. 11 A.M.–4 P.M., Sat. 11 A.M.–2 P.M. May–Nov., Tues.–Fri. 10 A.M.–4 P.M., Sat. 11 A.M.–2 P.M. Dec.–Apr., donations accepted), the best place to visit for local history. Don't miss the museum's *Sindia* display, commemorating the British ship that crashed off the 16th Street beach in the early 1900s with more than $1 million in valuables rumored to be onboard. Less than 25 years ago parts of the ship could still be seen in the water, but today it's completely submerged in sand.

Beaches

Beach tags cost $5 daily, $10 weekly, and $20 for the season. There are public restrooms at the Boardwalk Music Pier, and on First, Sixth, 12th, 34th, and 58th Streets. Remember, this is a dry town; no alcohol is allowed.

The city's best surfing beaches are at Seventh Street and 16th Street. Twenty-four free shuffleboard courts are located at Fifth Street and Boardwalk.

Events

Ocean City hosts dozens of events and activities during summer months, with additional events scheduled year-round. For more details call 609/525-9300.

The Cape's fine sand serves as a wonderful artistic medium, and Ocean City offers two chances to give your sculpting abilities a go. Though the first event takes place in July, I recommend you wait for the second, Ocean City's official August **Sand Sculpting Contest.** Starting at 9 A.M. on the Sixth Street beach, it's part of a day-long celebration culminating with the **Miss Crustacean Pageant,** a crowning of the year's most fetching hermit crab. No worries if your crab ain't a looker—there's also a hermit crab race.

Need a laugh? Check out April's annual **Doo Dah Parade.** Elvis impersonators and bagpipe blowers join more than 300 basset hounds as they wiggle their way down the street en route to the boardwalk's Music Pier. Comedy acts take center stage afterward. In May the city celebrates a seaside version of Groundhog Day with **Martin Z. Mollusk Day.** If hermit crab Martin sees his shadow, summer will come one week early. The celeb crustacean is joined by the Ocean City High School marching band, along with performance artist Suzanne Muldowney, also known as Shelley the Mermaid, or Underdog.

Find out which lucky lady wins a chance to be Miss America at June's **Miss New Jersey Pageant,** held at the boardwalk Music Pier. July's annual **Weekend in Venice** (609/525-9300) kicks off with the **Merchants in Venice Seafood Festival,** an evening of culinary delight held along downtown's Asbury Avenue. The following night, one of the world's longest boat parades takes place along the bay from the Longport Bridge to Tennessee Avenue. It's part of the **Night in Venice** celebration, and it's a sight to behold.

Candlelit **Ghost Tours of Ocean City** (9th St. and Asbury Ave., 609/814-0199, www .ghosttour.com, $14 adult, $8 child) are held nightly (except Sundays) throughout summer, beginning at 8 P.M. outside City Hall. Each tour includes approximately eight stops and lasts a little more than an hour. While stories are historically documented, ghost sightings aren't guaranteed.

The city's annual New Year's Eve **First Night** is one of New Jersey's best, a great way for families to ring in the new year together with plenty of local food and entertainment, including music by the Ocean City Pops Orchestra and the opening of Wonderland's rides.

Sports and Recreation

Entertaining families for nearly 50 years, family-owned **Gillian's Wonderland Pier** (6th St. and Boardwalk, 609/399-7082, www.gillians .com) is Ocean City boardwalk's main attraction, an indoor-outdoor amusement park with everything from a glass house to a swinging galleon. Some of the rides, such as the Musik Express, City Jet Coaster, and fire engines, have been here for more than 30 years, while others like the bumper boats and log flume, only a decade or two. Wonderland is home to a giant 140-foot Ferris wheel—the tallest structure in Ocean City—as well as a 1926 carousel with a ring dispenser. Grab the gold ring and win a free ride. Rides cost a designated number of tickets (usually 2–6), and tickets run $1 each. Special half-price and discount days are scheduled throughout the season. Just down the boards is **Gillian's Island Waterpark** (6th St. and Boardwalk, 609/399-7082, www .gillians.com, daily 9:30 A.M.–6 P.M. mid-June–Labor Day, $22 adult, $18 child for 3 hours), offering thrilling waterslides and prime ocean views. Go for a quick soak on Shotgun Falls, hop a double tube along Skypond Journey, or take a ride down the lazy river.

Along with Wonderland, **Playland's**

Castaway Cove (1020 Boardwalk, 609/399-4751, www.boardwalkfun.com) has been around in one form or another seemingly forever. The cove is replete with outdoor rides geared mostly towards a younger crowd, although a series of not-for-the-faint-hearted thrill rides have been added recently. There's a Tilt-A-Whirl, bumper cars, and an upside-down roller coaster, and for those with an iron stomach, a Gravitron centrifugal spinning machine. The indoor arcade is home to a shooting gallery and an old-school photo booth, as well as the best skee ball in town. The lanes have recently been updated with 100-point holes, but 270 points still wins a free game. The Cove opens daily at 1 P.M. from late June to Labor Day; check the website for shoulder-season hours. Ride tickets never expire. Playland's other boardwalk properties include **Pier 9 Miniature Golf & Speedway Go-Karts,** and the two-course **Golden Galleon Pirate's Golf** at 12th Street ($5.50–6.50). Just look for the bearded Muffler Man with an eye patch.

Manicured miniature golf courses are everywhere these days, but if you're missing the giant fiberglass frogs, pink elephants, and spinning octopuses of yesteryear, you'll find them on Ocean City's boardwalk. Though my favorite fairy-tale course was demolished (*sigh*) in the 1980s, there are still enough old-school courses to make this ol' salt proud. One of them is **Tee Time Golf** (7th St. and Boardwalk, 609/398-6763), just south of Wonderland Pier. Be sure to check out the course's bit of wall humor while waiting for your friend to make that final putt. **Goofy Golf** (920 Boardwalk, 609/398-9662) may be home to the only fiberglass Teenage Mutant Ninja Turtle still existing. Don't forget to call last on the final hole—you'll want to savor the opportunity for a free game.

Built in 1928, the Spanish-style **Music Pier** (825 Boardwalk, 609/525-9245) is one of the boardwalk's most recognizable structures, adorning postcards and picture books throughout the city. It's also Ocean City's prime entertainment venue, hosting annual events like the Miss New Jersey pageant and concerts throughout summer, and serves as home base for the **Ocean City Pops Orchestra** (www .oceancitypops.org).

Originally opened as a bowling alley around 1901, Ocean City's historic **Moorlyn Theater** (820 Boardwalk, 609/399-0006) is now a partially rebuilt four-screen movie theater. Entrance to the theater is on the side, just off the boardwalk. Five-screen seasonal **Frank's Strand Theatre** (9th St. and Boardwalk, 609/398-6565) is the boardwalk's only other movie theater. Built in 1938, it was the flagship location of New Jersey's Shriver Theater chain.

Bikes and surreys are permitted on Ocean City's boardwalk daily before 11 A.M., and there are plenty of places to rent them throughout summer. The city's flat terrain makes bikes a good option on streets as well—just use caution at the intersections. **Surf Buggy Center** has rental locations at Eighth Street and the boardwalk and 12th Street and the boardwalk. A one-week single-speed adult rental costs $45. Others to try are **Ocean City Bike Center** (740 Atlantic Ave., 609/399-5550) and **Oves Bike Rental** (4th St. and Boardwalk, 609/398-3712).

For kayak rentals try **Bay Cats** (316 Bay Ave., 609/391-7960, www.baycats.com), which also offers two-hour guided tours of Ocean City's back bay. Trips—ideal for birders and nature lovers—leave daily each morning throughout summer. Private sailing lessons aboard Hobie catamarans are also available. **Wet-n-Wild Waverunner Rentals** (3rd St. and Bay Ave., 609/399-6527, www.wetand wildwaverunners.com) offers personal watercraft for use on the bay, daily 9 A.M.–sunset Memorial Day–Labor Day.

Fishers cast their lines from the toll bridge over **Corson's Inlet** (609/861-2404, www.state.nj .us/dep/parksandforests/parks/corsons.html), a 341-acre park along Ocean Drive between Ocean City and Strathmere. Quiet and inspiring, the inlet is a great place for walking, and its waters are ideal for sailing and kayaking.

Accommodations
HOTELS
Ocean City is well equipped to handle overnight stays, with dozens of independent motor lodges, hotels, guesthouses, and inns. Although lodging is scattered throughout the city, the area around the Ninth Street Bridge offers the most selection.

Impala Island Inn (1001 Ocean Ave., 609/399-7500, www.impalaislandinn.com, $151–196) offers standard rooms with cable TV and a fridge, and some have additional sleeper sofas. To really feel like you're on vacation, request a room overlooking the pool.

Watson's Regency Suites (Ocean and 9th St., 609/398-4300, www.watsonsregency.com, $219–229 s, $289–309 d) features spacious efficiencies each with a balcony and ample closet space, and decorated in the pastel greens and pinks you'd expect at the Jersey Shore. It's a good choice for extended stays.

Rising from the boardwalk like a pink saltwater taffy is the towering **Port-O-Call** (15th St. and Beach, 609/399-8812, www.portocall hotel.com, $295–430), an Ocean City stalwart. Many of the hotel's rooms offer wonderful ocean views, and all include air-conditioning, TV, and use of the in-ground pool. For guests not quite ready to leave the beach, shower rooms are available after checkout.

Centrally located along the boards is the historic **Flanders** (719 11th St., 609/399-1000, www.theflandershotel.com, $339–980), a grand 1923 Spanish-style hotel featuring one- and two-room bedroom suites, recently added promenade suites with hardwood floors and Americana decor, and penthouse suites. The Flanders is a popular place for weddings, and apparently ghosts: It's rumored to be haunted.

B&BS AND GUESTHOUSES
Ocean City will never rival Cape May when it comes to B&Bs, but there are several treasures if you know where to look. In general, the city's guesthouses range from comfortable to constricting. Those on the higher end are listed below.

Operated by a California surfer, the **Koo-Koo's Nest Bed & Breakfast** (615 Wesley Ave., 609/814-9032, www.kookoosnest.com, $105–135) features themed guest rooms—my favorites are Caribbean Rooms 6 and 7—and suites, most with private baths and fridges. Rooms are small, but they're also a steal. The family-owned **Osborne's Fairview Inn** (601 E. 15th St., 609/398-4319, www.osbornesinn.com, $100–140 summer) offers a handful of small well-kept guest rooms and a few weekly rental apartments, all with TVs, fans, air-conditioning, and private baths. It's a simple beachy sort of place, just down the block from the boards.

The three-story **Scarborough Inn** (720 Ocean Ave., 800/258-1558, www.scarborough inn.com, $150–250) offers 24 individually styled guest rooms, along with a second-floor reading library and a sojourn room perfect for a game of Scrabble.

In the heart of downtown is **Atlantis Inn Luxury Bed & Breakfast** (601 Atlantic Ave., 609/399-9871, www.atlantisinn.com, $240–525), a suites-only Victorian originally built in 1905 and known for years as the Croft Hall Hotel, a vacationing home for Philadelphia's high society. The property was completely renovated in the early 2000s, transformed into 10 luxury suites and two apartments, each with a private bath, air-conditioning, a TV and DVD player, and access to an on-site spa offering hot-stone, deep-tissue, and Swedish massage. A spacious rooftop deck is ideal for winding out the day.

Most, if not all, of Ocean City's rental agencies cater to weekly or seasonal summer visitors. Some to try are **Grace Realty** (34th and Central, 800/296-4663), **Monihan Realty** (3201 Central Ave., 609/339-0998 or 800/255-0998, www.monihan.com), and **Berger Realty** (3160 Asbury Ave., 877/237-4371, www.bergerrealty.com).

Camping

Although it's a little more than a half-hour's drive to the beach, **Yogi Bear's Jellystone Park Camp-Resort** (1079 12th Ave., Mays Landing, 800/355-0264, www.atlanticcity jellystone.com) offers plenty to entertain kids—and their parents—without ever getting in the car. There's a playground, miniature golf course, and swimming pool, along with regular themed weekend celebrations mid-March–October—better pack your grass skirts and sneakers. No-hookup tent sites cost $37, and RV sites are $55. Barebones cabins ($100) and trailer rentals ($200) are also available.

Just three miles outside of Ocean City, **Whippoorwill Campground** (810 S. Shore Rd., Marmora, 609/390-3458 or 800/424-8275, www.campwhippoorwill.com, Apr.–Oct.) features sheltered wooded campsites along with an Olympic-size swimming pool, free hot showers, and themed events including Christmas in July and September's famed pig roast. Sites cost $50.50 per night based on two people.

Ten minutes from Ocean City is **Frontier Campground** (84 Tyler Rd., Ocean View, 609/390-3649, www.frontiercampground .com, mid-Apr.–mid-Oct.), a low-key place with shaded tent and RV sites. You'll find no bustling activities here—Frontier's all about relaxing. The campground also rents fully furnished "tree houses"—cabins on stilts—that each sleep five and include a kitchen ($100 for two people, $12 per night each additional adult). Basic campsites begin at $35 during the week.

Food

There's no room to argue: **Mack and Manco's** (609/399-2548, off-season hours typically 11:30–8:30 P.M. Mon.–Fri., until 10 or 10:30 P.M. Fri.–Sun., extended summer hours) serves the best slices of thin-crusted cheese pizza in existence. Ever. Take yours to go on a paper plate, grab a seat on a boardwalk bench, and devour it before the seagulls do. There are boardwalk locations at Eighth, Ninth (open year-round), and 12th Streets.

My dad never visits Ocean City without picking up a bucket of **Johnson's Popcorn** (1360 Boardwalk, 609/398-5404, www.johnsons popcorn.com), New Jersey's most delicious caramel corn hands-down. A bucket is large enough to last a week, but expect it to be gone in a day.

For an authentic Ocean City experience, start your day at **Oves** (5th and Boardwalk, 609/398-3712, www.ovesrestaurant.com), serving some of the best breakfast on the boardwalk, including apple cider doughnuts ($0.75) baked on-site. Request a table on the upper deck, but watch your food—the seagulls aren't shy. When you're through noshing, rent one of their bikes ($5 per hour) and ride off the calories. Oves also serves a selection of lunch eats and dinner entrées, specializing in seafood ($17–24).

Originating in Hawaii, **Hula Grill** (940 Boardwalk, 609/399-2400, www.hulagrill oc.com) opened its now-expanded eatery on the Ocean City boards in 1999. In addition to casual eats, the restaurant serves a selection of intriguing entrées inspired by its home state, including a heaping pulled-pork plate ($8) doused in Hula Grill's own barbecue sauce, and grilled ahi tuna with pineapple salsa ($15.75). The Grill is open full-time seasonally; call ahead for hours April–May and September–October.

Around since 1937, **The Chatterbox** (500 9th St., 609/399-0013, Sun.–Thurs. 7 A.M.–10 P.M., Fri.–Sat. 7 A.M.–11 P.M., $9–18) is an institution—the city's best place to come for a burger and fries or a bit of local nostalgia. **Luigi's Restaurant** (300 9th St., 609/399-4937, $12–21) has been serving up traditional Italian dishes in a cozy corner locale for decades.

Owners of the original 4th Street Café have relocated to Asbury Avenue, where they've opened **Who's on First!** (100 Asbury Ave., 609/399-0764, daily 6 A.M.–9 P.M., $15–25), an incarnation of their popular coffeehouse-eatery. A loyal clientele smitten with the homemade scones has followed. Stop by **Dixie Picnic** (819 8th St., 609/399-1999, www.dixie picnic.com) for your fill of upcakes—delish upside-down cupcakes with icing on all three sides. Get a dozen ($16) to go or one of your favorites (mine's chocolate malted devil's food cake) inside a box lunch with a sandwich, potato salad, and a deviled egg ($8.25). Hours are Monday–Thursday 7 A.M.–9 P.M., Friday–Saturday 7 A.M.–10 P.M. in summer, with additional hours year-round.

Downtown's recently opened **TigerLilly Café & The Courtyard** (805 E. 8th St.,

609/391-7777, $17–28) has brought a new caliber of dining to Ocean City. Healthy helpings of Southern-inspired breakfast, lunch, and dinner dishes that change regularly have put this place on the foodie map. The restaurant is located within the Homestead Hotel; call for hours.

Information and Services

Ocean City's **Information Center** (800/232-2465) is located outside the island, along Route 52 on the Stainton Memorial Causeway, just over the Ninth Street Bridge. Public restrooms are located at First, Sixth, 12th, 34th, and 58th Streets and the beach, and also at the Music Pier along the boardwalk. Most streets close to the boardwalk have metered parking. If you drive around long enough it's possible to find free parking spaces, though they're usually a hike from the action. There are several manned parking lots close to the boards, including a lot at Ninth Street and the boardwalk and another at Fifth Street and the boardwalk.

It's been said that Ocean City has never served a drop of alcohol, but this doesn't mean you can't bring some in. Several liquor stores are situated just outside the city's boundaries, making import ridiculously easy. Two to try are **Circle Liquor** (Somers Point, 609/927-2921), on the west side of the Ninth Street Bridge, and **Boulevard Super Liquors** (501 Roosevelt Blvd., 609/390-1300), across the 34th Street Bridge.

For beachgoers with limited mobility, surf wheel chairs can be rented by calling 609/525-9304. Advance reservations are suggested.

Getting There

Ocean City is 20 minutes south of Atlantic City. It's located off Garden State Parkway's Exits 30 or 25 (southbound) or Exits 25 or 29 (northbound).

SEA ISLE CITY AND STRATHMERE

While Sea Isle has long been a haven for college students and weekend renters who see Miller Lite as the epitome of Shore life, things in this city are changing. The number of families setting up year-round residence has increased dramatically, and the summer bungalows once prevalent throughout the island are coming down and being replaced by million-dollar homes. This shift has been stirring since the new millennium when Fun City—Sea Isle's only amusement center—was torn down, and quiet zones were implemented citywide to keep noise to a minimum. Sea Isle's heading in a calmer direction, true, but its party scene is still going strong.

Just north of the city is Strathmere, a thin stretch of land usually mistaken for an extension of Sea Isle. Along with several eateries and bars, Strathmere is home to one of the Jersey coast's only free beaches. Landis Avenue is the main route between Sea Isle City and Strathmere, and is part of the larger Ocean Drive route connecting Atlantic City with Cape May. It's also a major crossing route for endangered diamondback terrapins making their way to higher ground to lay eggs. The majority of these crossings take place in June and July, so keep an eye out for them. Stone Harbor's Wetlands Institute suggests when you see one crossing the road, pick her up and help her along.

Promenade

Sea Isle's oceanfront paved Promenade (often referred to as a boardwalk) plays host to a couple of casino arcades, several sweatshirt and trinket shops, and casual eateries serving burgers, pizza, and ice cream. The bulk of businesses are situated along the bottom floor of the Spinnaker condo complex on the Promenade's north end. A few blocks south is a **Boardwalk Casino Arcade** (42nd and Boardwalk, 609/263-1377) and **Gunslingers Old Time Photos** (43rd and Boardwalk, 609/263-4771, www.seaislephotography.com/oldtime), where donning garters, flasks, chaps, and boas makes a great 8-by-10 souvenir.

Sand dunes and shrubbery separate the 1.5-mile-long Promenade from the beach. Bicycling, in-line skating, and skateboarding are allowed on the walkway Monday–Friday 5 A.M.–3 P.M., summer weekends 5 A.M.–noon.

Beaches

Sea Isle's beach tags cost $5 daily, $10 weekly, and $20 for the season (quite a steal). Lifeguards are on duty daily 10 A.M.–5 P.M. throughout summer every few blocks—just walk until you find one. The city has several surfing beaches, including 26th Street, 42nd Street, 52nd Street, and 74th Street; rafting beaches at 24th Street, 45th Street, and 87th Street; and kayaking beaches at 30th Street, 56th Street, and 79th Street. Volleyball is allowed at 25th Street, 53rd Street, and 72nd Street, and surf fishing is allowed at the Townsend Inlet Bridge area south of 93rd Street and most city beaches north of 20th Street.

Entertainment and Nightlife

Cover bands and drink specials are the norm throughout Sea Isle. Most bars and clubs are open nightly in the summer months, but options diminish considerably during the off-season. The epitome of Sea Isle nightlife is the OD, or **Ocean Drive** (40th and Landis Ave., Sea Isle, 609/263-1000, http://theod.com, daily 10 A.M.–2 A.M. summer), centrally located just north of the island's causeway. The bar features a spacious dance floor, but that doesn't stop the place from packing wall-to-wall on weekends, especially when bands like **Love Seed Mama Jump** (http://loveseed.com) perform. Occasional events are hosted throughout the year.

The cavernous **Springfield Inn** (43rd and Pleasure Ave., Sea Isle, 609/263-4951, http://thespringfieldinn.com/main, Mon.–Fri. from 8 P.M., Sat.–Sun. from noon, summer) attracts a slightly older crowd with Wednesday trivia nights and half-price Heinekens. Its backyard open-air **Carousel Bar** (Mon.–Thurs. 11 A.M.–8 P.M., Fri.–Sat. 11 A.M.–10 P.M., Sun. noon–8 P.M.), adjacent to the Promenade, is the perfect place for sipping chill margaritas all afternoon. Just across the island causeway is **La Costa** (4000 Landis Ave., Sea Isle, 609/263-3611), a liquor store, lounge, and motel all rolled into one. The bar is known for its casual happy hour, but for something a bit more refined try the nearby **Dead Dog Saloon** (3809 Landis Ave., Sea Isle, 609/263-7600, http://seaislenightlife.com). This two-story tavern features a small menu of appetizers and sandwiches, along with live music, mixed drinks, and eight draft ales and stouts to choose from. Guys, if you want to enter after 6 P.M., make sure your shirt has a collar.

Plenty of people frequent **Braca Café** (Kennedy Blvd. and the beach, Sea Isle, 609/263-4271, www.bracacafe.com) for the food, but the property—which has belonged to the Braca family for more than a century—is best known to 20-somethings as the home of the 302, a mind-erasing mixture involving a Bacardi 151 double shot and a mean hangover.

Seasonal **Twisties Tavern** (232 S. Bayview Dr., Strathmere, 609/263-2200, www.twisties tavern.com, Wed.–Mon. noon–2 A.M. summer, closed Tues., $12–25) has never recovered from its speakeasy roots. A hidden bayside establishment revered among locals and virtually unknown to tourists, this wood-paneled bar and restaurant is as kitschy as it is kept. Nosh on scallops wrapped in bacon ($13) and fried calamari ($9.75) while admiring Twisties' mounted fish and chiseled coconut collections.

Sports and Recreation

Rent bikes and surreys, along with kayaks and surf chairs, at **Surf Buggy Center** (Kennedy Blvd. and Pleasure Blvd., Sea Isle, 609/628-0101 or 800/976-5679, www.surfbuggycenter .com). For more than 15 years **Sea Isle City Parasail** (86th St. and the bay, Sea Isle, 609/263-5555, www.seaisleparasail.com) has been lifting riders over ocean waters for spectacular views. On a clear day parasailers ($70 per person) can see all the way to Atlantic City. Boats depart from 86th Street and the bay every 1.5 hours throughout summer, beginning at 8 A.M.

Accommodations

Sea Isle's overnight options are limited. For more variety, head north into Ocean City or

set up outdoors at one the campground resorts west of the causeway bridge along Route 9.

The city's largest motel is **Sea Isle Inn** (6400 Landis Ave., Sea Isle, 609/263-4371, www.seaisleinn.com, $129–150), located at a busy intersection toward the island's south side. Rooms are standard, with TV, air-conditioning, a private balcony, and access to an outdoor swimming pool. The motel is next door to the lively **KIX McNutley's Bar** (www .kixmcnutleys.com), and both are better-suited for those preferring late nights to early mornings. Rates are less expensive with a stay of four or more nights.

Located one block from the beach, **The Colonnade Inn** (4600 Landis Ave., Sea Isle, 609/263-0460, www.thecolonnadeinn.com, $185–370) is a large Victorian guesthouse with 19 rentable rooms, ranging from studios to three-bedroom apartments, all with wireless Internet. Complimentary coffee and fresh baked goods are available each morning in the inn's great room.

Camping

Possibly home to New Jersey's largest number of campsites, **Ocean View Resort Campground** (2555 Rte. 9, 609/624-1675, www.ovresort .com, mid-Apr.–mid-Oct.) features 1,173 tent and RV sites on 180 wooded acres. Summer activities include clubhouse movies and a weekly Sunday flea market. The resort is located on the mainland just across Sea Isle's causeway bridge. Rates begin at $39 in early June, $59 late June–August. Lakeside sites cost extra.

On the mainland between Sea Isle and Ocean City, **Hidden Acres** (1142 Rte. 83, Cape May Court House, 609/624-9015 or 800/874-7576, www.hiddenacrescampground .com, mid-Apr.–mid-Oct., from $37) hosts 200 tent and RV sites and a freshwater lake for swimming. Two on-site rental cabins ($50–70) are also available.

Food

Several worthwhile seafood establishments are clustered around 43rd and the bay, but the finest of the bunch is **Mike's Seafood**

Market and Raw Bar (43rd and the bay, Sea Isle, 609/263-3458, www.mikesseafood.com, daily 9 A.M.–9 P.M. June–Aug., Sat.–Sun. 9 A.M.–9 P.M. off-season), voted best dock dining and best seafood raw bar by Sea Isle for nearly a dozen consecutive years. Start with a bucket of cheesy crab fries ($11), then settle in with a fresh steamed combo ($28) that includes large gulf shrimp, Nantucket sea scallops, and lobster tail. Directly behind the restaurant is **Mike's Crab Shack** (317 43rd St., Sea Isle, 609/263-1700), which along with grilled fish features salads and specialty wraps. Take note: Mike's is just as good to go.

Mildred's Strathmere Restaurant (Ocean Dr. and Prescott Rd., Strathmere, 609/263-8209, daily 4–10 P.M., $13–23) is one of the Shore's great old-school establishments, a cozy American restaurant that's been packing in crowds for more than 50 years.

For well over a century the upscale **Busch's Seafood** (8700 Anna Phillips Ln., Sea Isle, 609/263-8626, www.buschsseafood.com) has been feeding local denizens who flock here for the restaurant's signature crab dishes. Highlights include the crab imperial en casserole ($26.95) and Busch's famous she-crab soup ($7.50 per bowl), available Tuesdays and Sundays only. Dinner hours are Tuesday–Sunday from 4 P.M. late June–late September, closed Mondays. Call for additional hours.

Situated bayside at the foot of the inlet bridge is Strathmere's **Deauville Inn** (201 Willard St., Strathmere, 609/263-2080, www.deauvilleinn.com, $21–43), a local classic that's been drawing crowds with tasty American fare and summer weekly wings specials for years. Arrive by bike or by boat for bayside seating and brews along the beach. Monday–Saturday the Deauville opens at 11 A.M. year-round, Sunday at noon. Hungry for hotcakes? Hit up the '50s-themed **Shoobies Restaurant** (3915 Landis Ave., Sea Isle, 609/263-2000, call for hours, $7–17) in downtown Sea Isle. It's also a good spot for mint chocolate chip ice cream.

For late-night slices and pizza turnovers, try **Amici's** (38th and Landis Ave., Sea Isle, 609/263-2320, daily 11 A.M.–11 P.M., $7–24).

Their take-out window stays open until 3 A.M. summer weekends, and the restaurant's BYOB—so you can make a night of it. Bar crowds nurse their hangovers with hoagies from **McGowan's Food Market & Deli** (3900 Landis Ave., Sea Isle, 609/263-5500, daily 7 A.M.–8:30 P.M. summer, $6–9), home to the best sandwiches in Sea Isle.

Information and Services

Tourism information is available at www.seaisletourism.org and at Sea Isle City Chamber of Commerce (121 42nd St., 609/263-9090, www.seaislechamber.com).

Acme at 63rd and Landis Avenue is the island's only large supermarket.

Public restrooms are located along the Promenade at 32nd Street, 40th Street, and 44th Street; along the beach at 85th Street; and at Townsends Inlet Park Beach at 94th Street.

Getting There

Sea Isle is located off Garden State Parkway Exit 17 (southbound) or 13 (northbound).

AVALON AND STONE HARBOR

Seven Mile Island, a barrier island approximately four blocks wide, is home to the wealthy seaside towns of Avalon and Stone Harbor. While Stone Harbor especially is known for its enormous beachfront homes, both towns are surprisingly accessible, with affordable restaurants, interesting shops, and some of the Cape's best nightlife. They're also environmentally friendly. Avalon hosts some of the state's tallest sand dunes, an important plant-life habitat, while Stone Harbor is known for its commitment to wildlife habitat conservation.

Avalon's downtown stretches along Dune Drive between the Avalon circle and 33rd Street; Stone Harbor's commercial district centers around 96th Street and Third Avenue.

Wetlands Institute

Across Stone Harbor's causeway bridge lies the 6,000-acre Wetlands Institute (1075 Stone Harbor Blvd., 609/368-1211, www

.wetlandsinstitute.org, $7 adult, $5 ages 2–11), a series of salt marshes, boardwalks, viewing platforms, and educational facilities and programs pertaining to the conservation and preservation of coastal ecosystems. The institute offers opportunities for self-guided wetlands tours and birding, along with an indoor saltwater aquarium featuring horseshoe crabs, seahorses, and moon snails. There's also a touch tank for kids. The on-site **Tidewater Museum Store** is a great spot for picking up field guides, Wings n' Waters posters, and binoculars, and for viewing a revolving display of carvings by local artists.

The Wetlands Institute works extensively with the local population of diamondback terrapins, rescuing the eggs of injured females and raising them on-site before rereleasing them. The turtles—often casualties of Jersey Shore drivers, especially along Ocean Drive—can live up to 40 years if they manage to avoid predators and cars.

Field science classes, daylong trips, and kayaking camps are offered during summer for kids and high school students. Call 609/368-1211 for further details.

The center is open Monday–Saturday 9:30 A.M.–4:30 P.M. and Sunday 10 A.M.–4 P.M. mid-May–mid-October, Tuesday–Saturday 9:30 A.M.–4:30 P.M. mid-October–mid-May, with extended midweek hours during July and August.

Stone Harbor Bird Sanctuary

Stone Harbor's 21-acre Bird Sanctuary (114th St. and 3rd Ave., 609/368-5102) is finally becoming human-friendly. For years the sectioned-off forest at Stone Harbor's southern end was strictly limited to birds: blue and green herons, yellow-crowned egrets, songbirds, and lately, two families of willets. But plans are in the works to add walking trails and a spring-fed freshwater pond. The trails are expected to be finished sometime in 2009; docent-led tours will begin soon after.

Beaches

Daily beach tags run $6 daily, $12 weekly for those age 12 and older, and can be used for both Avalon and Stone Harbor. Avalon's surfing beach is the 30th Street beach, and there are several raft beaches, including 12th Street, 24th Street, and 61st Street. Beach access is limited between 43rd Street and 58th Street, where the borough's multimillion-dollar mansions bump up to the sand. Most are blocked from street view by towering trees but can be gawked at from the beach. Just follow the marked trails allowing public beach access at varying intervals.

Avalon beaches are annual nesting spots for two endangered bird species: piping plovers and least terns. To learn more, pick up a brochure at the Community Hall (30th St. and the beach).

Entertainment and Nightlife

Avalon and Stone Harbor host a few of the Cape's most popular live-music venues. Bands let loose on the outdoor deck of **Fred's Tavern & Liquor Store** (314 96th St., Stone Harbor, 609/368-5591, Mon.–Sat. 10 A.M.–2 A.M., Sun. noon–2 A.M.), while regulars toss back beers in Fred's darkened innards until the early morning hours.

Seasonal party spot and local stalwart **Jack's Place** (3601 Ocean Dr., Avalon, 609/967-5001, www.jacksavalon.com, May–Labor Day) is the best place for catching bands like Liquid A and Mr. Greengenes. Another favorite drink spot is the newly expanded **Princeton Bar** (2008 Dune Dr., Avalon, 609/967-3457, www.princetonbar.com), now with a bar and grill, tavern, and rock room. On summer nights the Princeton runs a door-to-door shuttle throughout Avalon (5–10 P.M.) with service to and from the establishment. You can either call for pickup (609/741-1117) or flag it down along Ocean Drive on weekends.

For an alcohol-free evening, catch a film at **Frank Theatre-Stone Harbor 5** (271 96th St., Stone Harbor, 609/368-7731), Seven Mile Beach's only movie theater.

Sports and Recreation

Avalon and Stone Harbor boast several worthwhile seasonal attractions, including the 18-hole **Pirate Island Golf** (27th St. and Dune

Dr., Avalon, 609/368-8344, www.pirate islandgolf.com, additional locations in Sea Isle and Ocean City), an elaborate seafaring-themed miniature golf course worthy of the Caribbean.

Stone Harbor paddle shop **Harbor Outfitters** (354 96th St., Stone Harbor, 609/368-5501, www.harboroutfitters.com) runs two-hour guided ecotours ($40 adult, $30 child) through local wetlands, including Hereford and Townsend's inlets, with evening full-moon tours throughout summer. The shop also sells stand-up paddleboards, used kayaks, and wave skis (a surfboard-kayak combo), rents out single ($20 per hour) and double ($30 per hour) kayaks, stand-up paddleboards ($50 per day), and surfboards ($35 per day), and offers various learning workshops throughout summer.

Rent bikes at Stone Harbor's family-owned **Harbor Bike & Beach Shop** (9828 3rd Ave., Stone Harbor, 609/368-3691, http://harborbike.com) between 98th and 99th Streets, or **Hollywood Bicycles** (2528 Dune Dr., Avalon, 609/967-5846, http://hollywoodbikeshop.com, closed Wed.) in Avalon.

Avalon is home to one of the East Coast's only high-dunes beaches. **The Wetlands Institute** (609/368-1211) hosts guided dune walks Wednesdays at 9 A.M. June–early September, leaving from the 48th Street dune path. Call for further details. The borough also hosts a half-mile beachfront walkway, which bicyclists are permitted to use daily 5–10 A.M.

Accommodations

The bulk of Seven Mile Island's overnight choices hover around 80th Street, where Avalon and Stone Harbor meet.

Now under new management, the 44-room **Avalon Inn Resort** (7929 Dune Dr., Avalon, 609/368-1543, www.avaloninn.org, $199–219) is a quiet motel with standard amenities and an outdoor pool.

Concord Suites (7800 Dune Dr., Avalon, 609/368-7800, www.concordsuites.com, May–Oct., $212) is Avalon's only all-suite hotel, a seasonal establishment about a one-block walk

to the beach. In addition to condo quarters, the hotel hosts an elevator, two swimming pools, and four sundecks.

Avalon's recently renovated **Windrift Hotel Resort** (80th St. and the beach, Avalon, 609/368-5175, www.windrifthotel.com, $230–310) provides overnight motel, efficiency, and condo accommodations, along with on-site amenities like an in-ground pool, a 50-foot oval bar, and a fun beach-garden patio perfect for evening cocktails. The hotel's restaurant offers an extensive American menu daily (breakfast–dinner).

In addition to superb ocean views and in-house Italian-inspired dining, Avalon's **Golden Inn Hotel & Resort** (Oceanfront at 78th St., 609/368-5155, www.goldeninn.com, $275–385) has a concierge who will book everything from sailing trips to parasailing equipment for you. If you can do without a view, the cost of a room is about $40 less.

Camping

On New Jersey's mainland just west of Avalon is **Avalon Campground** (1917 Rte. 9 N., Clermont, 609/624-0075 or 800/814-2267, www.avaloncampground.com, mid-Apr.–Sept.), offering wooded campsites for tents ($36) and RVs ($44–54). The campground also rents one- and two-bedroom log cabins ($80–90), and stationary trailers complete with air-conditioning and bathrooms ($1,025 weekly).

Food

Study the blackboard of daily offerings, then head right up to **Sea Grill's** (225 21st St., Avalon, 609/967-5511, www.seagrillrestaurant.com, daily from 5 P.M. year-round, $20–48) chef and place your steak or seafood order, along with a side or two. Despite the informalities, this ain't no fast-food place. One look at the wine list—and prices—will convince you otherwise.

Tiny BYO **Café Loren** (23rd St. and Dune Dr., Avalon, 609/967-8228, Tues.–Sun. 5:30–9 P.M., Memorial Day–Labor Day, $29–34) is a local fine-dining institution, serving first-rate meat and seafood dishes for more than 30 years.

Local breakfast haunt **Maggie's** (2619 Dune Dr., Avalon, 609/368-7422, daily from 6:30 A.M. summer, $7–12) serves French toast, omelets, and scrapple (yum!) along with lunch eats.

For fresh salads and banana-based smoothies, head to Stone Harbor's **Green Cuisine** (302 96th St., Stone Harbor, 609/368-1616, Mon.–Thurs. 10 A.M.–8 P.M., Fri.–Sun. 10 A.M.–8:30 P.M., $5–10), a nice alternative to the Shore's typical fried options.

Information and Services

Public restrooms are available at 10th St. and Dune Drive, Community Hall (30th St. and the beach, wheelchair accessible), the public safety building (31st St. and Dune Dr.), Borough Hall (32nd St. and Dune Dr.), and the tennis buildings (8th St. and 39th St.). There are public parking lots at 30th Street and Dune Drive, and 28th–20th Streets and the beach, among others.

Beach surf chairs for people with limited mobility can be rented through Avalon Beach Patrol (609/967-7587), or in Stone Harbor by phoning 609/368-5102.

Getting There

Avalon is located off Garden State Parkway Exit 13; for Stone Harbor, take Garden State Parkway Exit 10A (southbound) or 10B (northbound).

THE WILDWOODS

Collectively known as Wildwood-by-the-Sea or simply Wildwood, Five Mile Island consists of several towns, including North Wildwood, central Wildwood City, and southern Wildwood Crest. During the 1950s Wildwood earned the nickname "Little Vegas" due to its popularity as a vacation resort, party spot, and live-music venue. Bill Haley and His Comets publicly debuted "Rock Around the Clock" at the HofBrau Hotel at Atlantic and Oak Avenue; Chubby Checker performed his first twist at the Rainbow Club, just down the street; and

Bobby Rydell sang about his "Wildwood Days" on AM radio stations. Dick Clark even hosted *American Bandstand* from the Boardwalk's Starlight Ballroom during the summer months. At the same time hundreds of mom-and-pop motels sprung up around the island, most notably in Wildwood Crest, each trying to outdo the other with a more elaborate sign, higher-voltage lights, and plastic palm trees.

Sound tacky? That's what a lot of people thought, and the Wildwoods were pretty much left alone by investors and developers for years. Thankfully, this is what saved (or at least, postponed) Wildwood's affectionately dubbed doo-wop motels from destruction. Along with the boardwalk, it's these kitschy, campy structures that make Wildwood worth visiting in the first place. Now they're in danger, and so is Wildwood's allure.

Though the Wildwoods' "rediscovery" is evident in the upscale townhouses and condos popping up around the island and the demolition of doo-wop properties throughout, the place has managed to retain its working-class roots and remains the resort of choice for plenty South Jerseyans and Philadelphians.

Cheap eats, nightlife, and airbrushed fringed T-shirts are easy to come by, especially in Wildwood City, which feels more like a night at the fun house than a walk in the park. For now, the Wildwoods remain mostly seasonal, practically turning into a ghost town by late October and not kicking back in until May. Most restaurants and some hotels completely shut down for the winter, although come June you'll think the whole tristate region moved to town.

◖ Boardwalk

There is nothing quite like the Wildwood two-mile boardwalk, a smorgasbord of T-shirt shacks, gyro stands, arcades, amusements—one big buildup of color and kitsch. This extended carnival stand is one of New Jersey's best people-watching spots. In fact, there's little you won't find on these boards: Garlic fries, funnel cakes, giant stuffed Looney Tunes dolls, airbrushed T-shirts, and painted hermit crabs are all here, along with proph-esizing iron-ons and temporary tattoos. Tramcars carrying weary vacationers up and down the walkway play pre-recorded warnings that'll stick with you all summer: "Watch the tram car, please. *Please,* watch the tram car." Though the Wildwoods are currently under-going gentrification, this doesn't hold true for the boardwalk. Black, white, and Latino fami-lies, couples, and teens all fit in perfectly. I can't imagine it any other way.

One of the boardwalk's best attractions are its infamous **tram cars,** running the walk-way's length in a continuous loop and picking up worn vacationers as they go. It seems these vehicles will stop for no one, so heed those warnings and "wa-wa-watch the tram car" or you may find you've become another board-walk attraction. The transport stops wherever you like and costs $2 each way, although to-kens will soon be required to pay.

Another great Wildwood staple is the mul-tilevel **Boardwalk Mall** (3800 Boardwalk, 609/522-4260), the perfect shopping spot for flimsy gold rings, Hawaiian-print totes, and that Johnny Depp poster you've been pin-ing for.

Ladies and gentleman, you ain't seen noth-ing like the boardwalk's **Seaport Aquarium** (3400 Boardwalk, 609/522-2700, $7–8 adult, $6–7 child), or so the employee standing out-side with a live serpent draped over his neck would have you believe. This small attraction is home to several shark species, including lemon, sand tiger, and nurse sharks, along with alli-gators, crocs, pythons, and piranhas. It's just what you'd expect in Wildwood.

Amusement Piers

Wildwood's amusement piers are famous, at least around the Mid-Atlantic. These aren't all kiddie lands, mind you. This is serious stuff! The Morey family (www.moreyspiers.com), developers of the Wildwoods' first amuse-ment pier, currently owns all three in operation as well as two beachfront water parks. Passes bought for one can be used at any, although some rides require an additional fee.

© LAURA KINIRY

Step right up and win a prize at Wildwood's famous boardwalk.

Situated at Spencer Avenue and the boardwalk, **Adventure Pier** hosts some of the boardwalk's most adrenaline-inducing rides, including one of the state's best roller coasters, the **Great White.** This wood and steel hybrid runs at 50 miles per hour and reaches heights of more than 100 feet. Additional rides include a human slingshot and the Inverter, carrying 24 people at a time up 50 feet and inverting them before returning to the ground. There's also a carousel, the kids-only Apache Helicopters, and the disorienting Chamber of Checkers, sort of like a glass house, but different.

For more excitement hit **Surfside Pier,** home to **AtmosFEAR,** a free-fall tower that keeps riders in the dark, literally. The pier recently updated its **Great Nor'easter Roller Coaster** with Freedom Flight seats—suspended seats placing riders on the outer loop. The coaster winds above Ocean Oasis Waterpark and does a double spin at up to 50 miles per hour. Surfside Pier is also home to a Formula 1 raceway, rideable for an additional fee, along with more than two dozen kid-friendly amusements and Dante's Dungeon, the boardwalk's obligatory dark ride.

Mariner's Landing Pier has gathered together some of the boardwalk's best rides, including the Pirates of the Wildwood's 3-D adventure and the **Giant Wheel,** an open-car 156-foot Ferris wheel that's one of the tallest in the state. At night the wheel lights up with over 200,000 LED bulbs. Mariner's Landing also features a climbing wall, paddleboats, bumper cars, and the Sea Serpent upside-down roller coaster.

Access to all Morey Piers is free, although rides are paid for through the purchase of wristbands or EZ tickets, which deduct individual ticket costs with each ride. A one-day wristband for all three piers costs $45 adult, $33 child. An EZ pass runs $50 for 70 tickets, $25 for 30.

Situated at the back of Surfside Pier is **Ocean Oasis Waterpark & Beach Club,** where you'll find a kid-friendly activity pool with walkable lily pads and a climbing cargo net, a lazy river, and high-speed waterslides like Riptide Rapids and Sidewinders, two side-by-side slides that twist and turn while dropping 40 feet. Mariner's Landing **Raging Waters** features a rope swing, a Skypond Journey into four different elevated pools, and a Camp KidTastrophe equipped with water guns and water sprays. An all-day admission to both water parks is $33 adult, $25 child. Three hours at one water park costs $28 adult, $20 child.

A third Wildwood water park, this one visible from Wildwood streets, is the colorful **Splash Zone** (Schellenger Ave. and the boardwalk, 609/729-5600, www.splashzonewaterpark.com). The park has more than a dozen slides, rides, and attractions, including the Beast of the East, the Mid-Atlantic's only six-person raft ride; the torpedo-like Terminator; and a giant bucket that empties 1,000 gallons of water on park-goers every three minutes. A three-hour pass is $26 adult, $20 child, and an all-day pass goes for $28–30 adult, $21–24 child.

Other Sights

Just across the bridge from Stone Harbor is North Wildwood's **Hereford Inlet Lighthouse** (1st and Central Ave., 609/522-4520, www.herefordlighthouse.org, daily 9 A.M.–5 P.M. mid-May–mid-Oct., Wed.–Sun. 10 A.M.–4 P.M. mid-Oct.–mid-May, $4 adult, $1 child), a still-active Victorian lighthouse built in 1874. With five indoor fireplaces and English gardens that attract hundreds of butterflies annually, the property feels less like a lighthouse and more like that of a country home. Visitors are invited to tour the lighthouse and indoor museum, which includes the light's original whale-oil lamp. It's free to browse the gardens and gift shop. For those also planning a trip to nearby Cape May's lighthouse, combination tickets can be purchased at Hereford ($9 adult, $3 child under 11).

Beaches

Sure, the beaches are free. But at a half mile in width, it takes work to enjoy them. Really, it's not *so* bad. Benches are scattered along about midway from the ocean, offering nice respite for weary or scorched feet. Playgrounds, volleyball nets, and shuffleboard courts are also set up along the sand, notably alongside the boardwalk. North Wildwood's Moore's Inlet is the Wildwoods' only beach allowing dogs and barbecues. It's also a great spot for fishing and personal watercraft use.

There's a surfing beach between Eighth and 10th Avenues in North Wildwood, and another at Rambler Road in Wildwood Crest.

Festivals and Events

Since opening in 2002, the doo-wop-inspired **Wildwoods Convention Center** (4501 Boardwalk, 609/846-2631 or 800/992-9732) has brought the island new life by hosting close to 500 events each year, including October's annual **Fabulous '50s Weekend** (www .gwcoc.com), with musical performances by the likes of Ben E. King and the Del Vikings, and April's annual **Sensational '60s Weekend** (www.gwcoc.com), complete with a record hop deejayed by local radio icon Jerry "The Geator" Blavat.

Wildwood's long-running **National Marbles Tournament** (301/724-1297, www .nationalmarblestournament.org) occurs each June at a permanent beach location in front of the boardwalk. More than 1,000 games are played over the four-day tournament. You can also visit the city's **Marbles Hall of Fame** at the **George F. Boyer Historical Museum** (3907 Pacific Ave., 609/523-0277).

Held annually over Memorial Day weekend, the **Wildwood International Kite Fest** (Cresse Ave.–Burk Ave. on the beach and Wildwood Convention Hall, 609/729-4000, www.gwcoc .com) is the country's largest, featuring world-renowned kite builders, kite-making workshops and exhibits, and an illuminated Night Kite Fly. Kite Ballet, a takeoff on figure skating, is one of the weekend's more serious events—fliers come prepared for all weather conditions.

Recreation and Entertainment

Wildwood Crest's beachfront **Promenade** offers welcome relief from its northern boardwalk neighbor. Much more low-key, it's a

© LAURA KINIRY

the Wildwoods Convention Center

good stretch for jogging or beach cruising. If you haven't brought your own ride, rent one at **Bradley's Bikes** (Rambler Rd. and Ocean St., 609/729-1444) across the street from the Admiral's Quarters restaurant. Bikes are allowed on the boards daily 5–11 A.M.

The borough's **New Jersey Surf Camps** (Ocean Outfitters, 6101 New Jersey Ave., 609/729-7400, www.newjerseysurfcamps.com) offers private ($45 per hour) and group surfing lessons for all ages year-round. A one-day surf "camp" runs $65 (weekdays 9:30 A.M.–noon or 2:30–5 P.M.), or spend the entire weekend catching waves (Sat.–Sun. 9–11 A.M., $130).

Atlantic Parasail Inc. (1025 Ocean Dr., 609/522-1869, www.atlanticparasail.com, $65 per person) offers tandem and single-harness rides above the ocean.

Billed as the world's fastest speedboat, the 70-foot-long, 147-passenger *Silver Bullet* (609/522-6060, www.silverbullettours.com) shoots across Wildwood waters at exhilarating speeds. Ninety-minute rides depart from the Wildwood Marina (Rio Grande and Susquehanna Aves.).

Accommodations

Many of Wildwoods' motels remain so old-school they're still advertising cable TV. This is a good thing, at least in theory. Motels and amusements are this Shore resort's top two attractions, but not many people want to stay in tiny rooms without hair dryers and central air when there's a fancy hotel up the street. That's why the best of Wildwood's bunch is upgrading and updating while keeping the funky neon signs, plastic palm trees, and 1950s flair that made them attractive in the first place. And if they're family-owned, even better. Book a room in a good Wildwood motel (and there are plenty of bad ones, believe me) and you're in for one of the most unique experiences along the Jersey Shore, let alone the country. Sure, such far-out places were all over the United States 50 years ago, but not anymore. Even in these parts doo-wop is endangered, so do your part to keep it around. Dig?

A good choice for families looking to spend time on the boardwalk, downtown Wildwood's **Le Voyageur Motel** (232 Andrews Ave., Wildwood, 609/522-6407, $99–175) offers standard motel rooms and efficiencies and hosts several outdoor decks, along with a heated pool. Known for its cleanliness, the two-part doo-wop-certified **Heart of Wildwood** (3915 Ocean Ave., Wildwood, 609/522-4090, www.heartofwildwood.com, $125–180) features both a 44-unit boardwalk location and a 30-room motel diagonally across the street on Ocean Avenue. All rooms are smoke-free, with air-conditioning, TVs, and DVD players. Both have heated pools *and* plastic palm trees.

With its plastic palms, angular roof, and kidney-shaped pool, the **Caribbean** (5600 Ocean Ave., Wildwood Crest, 609/522-8292, www.caribbeanmotel.com, $141–199) is a doo-wop classic—it's actually listed on the National Register of Historic Places. The motel has been completely renovated and revamped with an updated 1950s style: Its lounge combines

the neo-doo-wop Starlux Motel, Wildwood City

leopard-print furnishings with boomerang tables and complements them with a flat-screen TV; and guest rooms feature modern amenities enhanced by tropical-striped linens and lime rickey walls. And with shuffleboard and a panoramic sundeck, this place is hard to beat. Situated along the beach in Wildwood Crest, the seasonal **Fleur de Lis Resort Motel** (6105 Ocean Ave., Wildwood Crest, 609/552-0123, www.fleurdelismotel.com, May–mid-Oct., $130–366) features three stories of clean rooms, each with a kitchenette, air-conditioning, and wireless Internet. Highlights include a sundeck overlooking both the pool and the beach, and a game room with Ping-Pong.

It's impossible not to love North Wildwood's **Lollipop Motel** (23rd and Atlantic Aves., North Wildwood, 609/729-2800, www.lollipop motel.com, $189–217), if only for its roadside cherub-faced taffy sign and its candy-colored doors. Add to that Wi-Fi, a heated pool with a diving board, a patio with barbecue grills, and recently renovated rooms complete with kitchenettes, and you may find yourself gushing.

From its exterior, **The Pan American Hotel** (5901 Ocean Ave., Wildwood Crest, 609/522-6936, www.panamericanhotel .com, $186–240) looks *so* Miami Beach. There are palm trees (sh-h-h…plastic), private balconies, and a flashy ice-blue color scheme, along with a circular swimming pool that's as inviting as a Skyy martini. But head inside and this neo-doo-wop property is Wildwood all the way. There's nothing wrong with the Deja Blue rooms, but it's the renovated Summer Breeze rooms that'll make a doo-wop convert out of you, if you're not already.

Right on the beach, the family-friendly **Armada by-the-Sea** (6503 Ocean Ave., Wildwood Crest, 609/729-3000, www.armada motel.com, $182–335) is one of Wildwood's larger doo-wop properties, a three-story motel with pleasant rooms and an elevator, in the quiet part of town. Accommodations—ranging from single rooms to three-room suites—all have balconies with partial ocean views, along with microwaves and fridges. Armada's best

feature (besides its neon sign) is its Olympic-size heated pool, the perfect place for a swim while acclimating.

The first of Wildwood's neo-doo-wop properties, **◖ Starlux Motel** (305 E. Rio Grande Ave., 609/522-7412, www.thestarlux.com, $219–339) is the reincarnated former Wingate Motel, complete with an elevator, a whirlpool, and a hip modern take on the city's signature style. Designers salvaged throwaways from demolished doo-wop properties and recycled them into room furnishings and fabrics, complementing additional touches like lava lamps and Technicolor color schemes. Rooms are still small, but are much more of an experience. Besides, you can always spend your days at the heated pool or property's all-glass Astro Lounge. The motel also offers a couple of renovated Airstream trailers for overnight stays.

Camping

About 10 minutes west of Wildwood, **Acorn Campground** (Rte. 47, Green Creek, 609/886-7119, www.acorncampground.com, late May–early Sept., $40–45) features 330 wooded sites for tents and RVs. Perks include free hot showers, two swimming pools, and two license-free fishing ponds. At nearby **King Nummy Trail Campground** (205 Rte. 47 S., Cape May Court House, 609/465-4242, www.kingnummytrail .com, late Apr.–Oct.) families can throw horseshoes, compete at shuffleboard, or play badminton. Tent and RV sites run $32–36, and on-site cabins $50–90.

Food and Nightlife

While not a culinary hotspot, the Wildwoods hold their own when it comes to local favorites. Wildwood City's Schellenger Avenue hosts a couple of restaurants, including the kitschy **Schellenger's Restaurant** (3516 Atlantic Ave., Wildwood, 609/522-0533, daily from 3 P.M. summer, $15–29). Known as "Lobster City," this seasonal space serves seafood-heavy American eats in a nautically themed setting. You can't miss it: just look for the fiberglass lobster and a rooftop seaside-inspired menagerie. **Neil's Steak and Chowder House** (222

THE WILDWOODS' DESIGNS ON DOO-WOP

Wildwoods' motel boom happened in the 1950s, when autos ran rampant but air travel wasn't as ubiquitous as it is today. Americans were glimpsing faraway places on TV but didn't have the time or means to reach them. In stepped North Wildwood, Wildwood, and Wildwood Crest, beachside motels began evoking far-off places like Hawaii and Singapore, appealing to local families who wanted to feel like they were truly getting away. Most of these establishments were mom-and-pop-owned, ordinary cement buildings with smallish rooms and efficiencies. So in order to differentiate themselves from one another, they added oversize flashy neon signs, angular roofs, kidney-shaped pools, exotic themes (evident in larger-than-life names like Pink Champagne, Monaco, and Caribbean Breeze), "perks" like air-conditioning and television, and parking spots only a few feet away from the door. The kitschy decor ranged from pirate statues to futuristic motifs.

While it's true such places were popular throughout the United States, many are long since gone, either rebuilt as condos or replaced by homes. However, the Wildwoods were all but forgotten during much of the 1980s and 1990s, a lack of commercial attention that left these tacky jewels as diamonds in the rough just waiting to be uncovered.

In 1997 the late architect Steve Izenhour did just that. A proponent of Vegas-style kitsch (the Wildwoods were often referred to as "Little Vegas" during the 1950s), Izenhour was en-

amored with the Wildwoods' wacky motels and first used the term "doo-wop" in talking about the Wildwoods' architectural offerings. (This style is also known as "populuxe," "California googie," and "Jetsonian" in other parts of the country.) Together with one of the Wildwoods' great founding sons, Jack Morey, Izenhour developed the **Doo Wop Preservation League**

Cherubic faces welcome visitors to the Lollipop Motel, North Wildwood.

E. Schellenger Ave., Wildwood, 609/522-5226, daily 4:30–10 P.M. summer, Fri.–Sat. 4:30–9:30 P.M. shoulder seasons, $15–26) is a popular surf-and-turf where customers dine in dark wood booths under Tiffany-style lampshades. Free parking and an early-bird special are big draws.

Housed in a seemingly unlucky location along Atlantic Avenue, **Jersey Girl** (3601 Atlantic Ave., Wildwood, Wed.–Mon. 5 P.M.–midnight summer, closed Tues., 609/522-7747) is the newest incarnation in a long line

of eateries, including Maureen's, Blue Olive, and Red Sky Cafe. The restaurant serves Shore classics like stuffed flounder ($20) and jumbo crab cakes ($20), along with pastas and specialty sandwiches. In keeping with one of the former establishments' themes, Jersey Girl offers a superb martini selection that alone is worth your visit.

Locals recommend Wildwood Crest's **Admiral's Quarters** (7200 Ocean Ave., Wildwood Crest, 609/729-1133, daily 7 A.M.–2 P.M. summer, $7–12) for omelets and (www.doowopusa.org), a nonprofit aimed at highlighting and protecting the Wildwoods' unique architectural contribution.

Unfortunately, the league was formed just as the Wildwoods were being rediscovered as a beach resort, but not for their pop-culture attractions. As Preservation League members were attempting to inspire businesses to promote the doo-wop spirit, dozens of motels were meeting the wrecking ball, and what was once the largest collection of "midcentury commercial" architecture found in one place quickly began disappearing. Today the trend continues. Doo-wop is out of style, man, lacking many of the modern amenities that other Shore towns offer. Money is talking, and many motel owners are taking the more lucrative road when faced with the choice between selling or investing millions in a property that needs a complete overhaul.

In 2005, more than half of the Wildwoods' doo-wop properties had already been demolished; at the same time, local chain and independent businesses garnished themselves with doo-wop accessories, including the Harley Davidson shop and the Wawa convenience store along Rio Grande Avenue, as well as the Wildwood Convention Center, now featuring giant beach balls and a doo-wop-style sign out front. The entire doo-wop motel district was listed as one of **Preservation New Jersey's** (www.preservationnj.org) Ten Most Endangered Sites for 2005, and the area has been nominated for listing on the New Jersey State Register of Historic Places. The Caribbean became the first of the motels to gain an official historic listing in July 2005.

For those interested in doo-wop, there are a number of outlets. The Doo Wop Preservation League runs a doo-wop architectural bus tour through the Wildwoods' streets evenings June-August. Tickets ($10 adult, $5 child) may be purchased at the **Wildwood Convention Center** (4501 Boardwalk, 609/729-9000) ticket office, and buses leave across the street from in front of the new **Doo Wop Museum** (3201 Pacific Ave., 609 729-4000), home to a garden of neon signs preserved from former doo-wop properties, along with a café and a malt shop. Contact the Doo Wop Preservation League (609/729-4000, info@doowopusa. org) for further tour details and times. Doo-wop fans may also want to check out the 2003 documentary *Wildwood Days* by filmmaker Carolyn Travis, who spent her childhood summers vacationing in Wildwood. The movie is a nostalgic look into the Wildwoods' past and is heavy on the doo-wop shots. A book highlighting Wildwoods doo-wop with excellent color photos, Kirk Hasting's **Doo Wop Motels: Architectural Treasures of the Wildwoods,** is available at area bookstores. In addition, the **Wildwood Crest Historical Society** (116 E. Heather Rd., 609/729-4515, www.cresthistory.org) offers some information on the borough's doo-wop history, and visitors can pick up a map of current and former doo-wop properties at the Doo Wop Museum.

short stacks. The restaurant is tucked away on the bottom floor of the Admiral Resort Motel. Perhaps the Wildwoods' finest restaurant, upscale **Marie Nicole's** (9510 Pacific Ave., Wildwood, 609/522-5425, www.marienicoles .com, daily 5–10 P.M., closed Tues., $21–34) serves eclectic American cuisine in an intimate setting, with both a bar and a glass-enclosed dining room. Dishes include New Zealand rack of lamb ($34) and lemongrass encrusted ahi tuna ($29).

Looking for an authentic boardwalk snack?

Order a cup of fresh-cut **Curley's Fries** (822 Boardwalk, 609/398-4040, $5) with a side of cheese dip. C'mon, it's the Shore! For something a little more substantial, **Mack's Pizza** (4200 Boardwalk, 609/729-0244) serves the best slices in town. Just off the boardwalk is the bright pink **Laura's Fudge** (Wildwood and Ocean Aves., 609/729-1555, www.laurasfudgeshop.com), Wildwood's name in fudge since 1926.

For nightlife with your meal, stick to Wildwood and North Wildwood, where food is good and drinks are plenty. With a bit o' Irish luck you'll score a stool at **Tucker's Pub** (3301 Atlantic Ave., Wildwood, 609/846-1110, www.tuckers-pub.com) before the crowd packs in. Guinness, Harp, and Smithwicks are the resident beers, and the food recently got an upgrade with a new executive chef. Platters include shepherd's pie ($15) and bangers and mash ($13). At **Goodnight Irene's** (Poplar and Pacific Aves., Wildwood, 609/729-3861, www.goodnightirenes.com, daily 11 A.M.–3 A.M.) choose from dozens of draft beers and 60 in bottles, including Philadelphia Brewing Walt Wit, Landshark Lager, and Smuttynose Old Brown Dog Ale. Irene's also serves a menu of brick-oven pizzas with toppings like cheese steak and buffalo chicken. There are daily drink and dining specials throughout the week.

For a full-service waterfront meal or casual bayside dining, stop by the **Boathouse** (Rio Grande Ave., Wildwood, 609/729-5301, www.boathouseonline.net, $15–23) at the foot of the Rio Grande Bridge. In addition to a menu of meat and seafood entrées, along with deck dishes such as hot dogs ($3.25) and bacon cheeseburgers ($6.75), the Boathouse offers an interesting selection of frozen drinks, including the rum-spiked multifruit Tropicana and a mudslide made with Bailey's, ice cream, Kahlua, and vodka. Looks like you'll be spending the night. The Boathouse marina deck is open Tuesday–Thursday 11:30 A.M.–11 P.M., Friday–Saturday 11:30 A.M.–midnight. The dining room is open nightly 4–10 P.M. Call for off-season hours.

Information and Services

The **Great Wildwoods Tourism Improvement and Development Authority** is an umbrella organization for Wildwood City, Wildwood Crest, and North Wildwood, offering tourism info and hosting numerous events throughout the summer season. For more information, call 800/992-9732 or visit www.wildwoodsnj.com.

The **Greater Wildwood Hotel Motel Association** (800/786-4546 or 609/522-4546, info@wildwoods.org, www.wildwoods.org, Mon.–Fri. 9 A.M.–5 P.M., Sat.–Sun. 10 A.M.–2 P.M. summer, call for off-season hours) hosts an information center stocked with maps and brochures pertaining to the Wildwoods' motels, restaurants, and attractions. It's located on the south side of Route 47, just west of Wildwood.

Getting There and Around

Wildwood is accessible from Exit 4B southbound or Exit 4 northbound of the Garden State Parkway. You can also get here by taking Ocean Drive south from Stone Harbor or north from Cape May, and from the greater Philadelphia region by traveling Route 55 to Route 47 and continuing east into Wildwood City.

Cape May and Vicinity

What began as a prosperous 17th-century whaling town grew into the nation's "most famous seaside resort" by the 1850s, hosting such luminaries as Abraham Lincoln, Benjamin Harrison, and Franklin Pierce. Today, with its gaslit streets, horse-drawn carriages, and over 600 gingerbread Victorians, Cape May feels like a step back in time. But it wasn't always so: The city's architecture was considered outdated by the 1970s, and vacationers were bypassing Cape May for more modern towns like Ocean City and Beach Haven. Still, a group of concerned citizens and preservationists fought to use the city's Victorian excess to its advantage. There's no question as to whether it worked. Cape May's now home to more than 80 bed-and-breakfasts, along with dozens of tours, events, and festivals that center around the Victorian theme. And with the state's most moderate temperatures, Cape May's become a 10-month destination—a beachside resort as popular

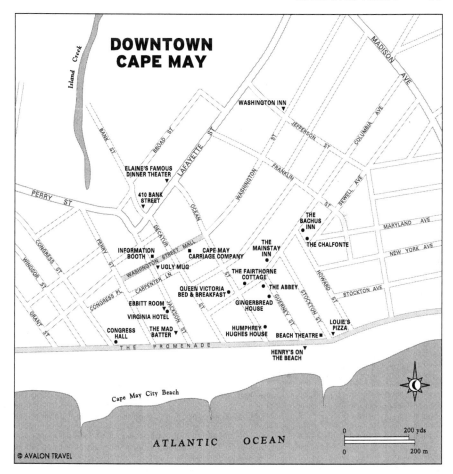

DOWNTOWN CAPE MAY

in December as in July. The city closes up shop come January, trickling to a start again in mid-February and slowly adding hours until summer's full schedule. Some of the best months for a Cape May visit are April–May and September–October, when there are fewer crowds and lower prices, and most of the shops and restaurants are still open. The winter holidays are also a great time to experience Cape May. It's cold as heck, but there are enough activities like candlelight house tours, heated trolley rides, and fireside cider drinks to make it all worthwhile.

SIGHTS
The Emlen Physick Estate

In 1970, on the verge of being demolished and replaced by modern homes, the Cape May Cottagers Association stepped in and saved the four-acre Physick Estate (1048 Washington St., 609/884-5404 or 800/275-4278, www.capemaymac.org) from the wrecking ball. Today, the estate is home to the very preservation group that spared it, though they now go by the name Mid-Atlantic Center for the Arts (MAC). Former home of Dr. Emlen Physick, a "father of American surgery" descendant, the

gingerbread architecture, Cape May

late-18th-century 18-room Victorian mansion and its surrounding property are Cape May's crowning jewels, a highlight on local trolley rides and Christmas tours and a centerpiece for festivals and events. The mansion's exterior is graced with exaggerated inverted chimneys and other unique adornments, while indoors are finely furnished Victorian rooms and changing exhibits on 18th-century life. The estate's Carriage House hosts a rotating gallery of art, along with the **Twinings Tea Room** (609/884-5404, ext. 138), serving a selection of finger foods, snacks, and sandwiches.

Tours of the estate ($10 adult, $5 child) take place daily 10:30 A.M.–3 P.M. May–October, daily 11 A.M.–3 P.M. November–December, and Friday–Saturday 11 A.M.–2 P.M. in January and March. Call for February hours. Two-hour combination trolley and estate tours ($18 adult, $9 child) are also available.

The Promenade

Lining Ocean Avenue's beachfront, Cape May's Promenade is home to a couple of arcades and some wonderful breakfast eateries. Look for **Morrow's Nut House** (609/884-4966), which sells warm roasted nuts and red fish candies perfect for snacking on a nearby bench, where the ocean view is unbeatable.

BEACHES

Cape May's beach tags cost $4 per day or $9 for three days. A season pass costs $25. Children 12 and under can use the beach for free. Beach chairs and umbrellas are available for rent right on the beach.

FESTIVALS AND EVENTS

As with the bulk of Cape May's tours, many of the city's events are sponsored by the Mid-Atlantic Center for the Arts.

Attending September's annual four-day **Cape May Food and Wine Festival** is a great way to sample the city's many culinary treats. Highlights include a gourmet marketplace with a people's choice chowder contest, a winery cellar tour, and a multiple-course beer-tasting dinner.

Since 2001 the **Cape May New Jersey**

State Film Festival (609/884-6700, www .njstatefilmfestival.com) has been drawing November crowds to the city for multiple-day showings of independent films, documentaries, shorts, and kids' cinema. Screenings take place throughout town at such venues as the Beach Theatre and Congress Hall.

For a true Victorian experience, nothing beats one of Cape May's **Sherlock Holmes Weekends** (609/884-5404 or 800/275-4278, www.capemaymac.org) held annually in March and November. Each sleuthing adventure features a cast of characters, including local turn-of-the-20th-century businessman John Wanamaker, as well as Holmes and his partner, Watson. Though period costumes aren't mandatory, there are prizes awarded for the best. Saturday's search for clues carries participants through some of the city's finest structures, and tickets for this event ($15) are sold separately for those who can only afford—both literally and figuratively—a couple of hours. If stepping back into a Victorian weekend is too short a time, visit Cape May during October's

Victorian Week (609/884-5404 or 800/275-4278, www.capemaymac.org), 10 days of antique shows, house tours, interactive murder mysteries, costume, dance, and a Victorian fashion show.

SHOPPING

Most Cape May shopping takes place along **Washington Street Mall** (609/884-2133, www.washingtonstreetmall.com), a pedestrian-only brick-paved stretch lined by specialty stores and restaurants. Antique items, lighthouse collectibles, Cape May logo hoodies, beach apparel, and footwear are in great supply here as well as within shops along the city's side streets. Stop by **Atlantic Books** (500 Washington St., 609/898-9694, www.atlanticbooks.us) for books on Cape May lore or trade paperbacks, then cross the mall to **Zoo Company** (421 Washington St., 609/884-8181, www.cape maypuppets.com) for inexpensive Schleich-made Smurfs and Hello Kitty mirrors. If you like to eat (and who doesn't?), why not show appreciation for the one who feeds you with a

© LAURA KINIRY

Washington Street Mall, Cape May

gift from **Love the Cook** (404 Washington St., 609/884-9292, www.lovethecook.com). **The Original Fudge Kitchen** (513 Washington St., 609/884-8814, www.fudgekitchens.com) almost always has an employee or two handing out free samples, but for a more substantial sweet **Dellas 5 & 10** (501-503 Washington St., 609/884-4568, www.Dellas5and10.com) features a back-of-the-store old-fashioned soda fountain serving sundaes, shakes, and floats, and **Uncle Charley's** (306 Washington St., 609/884-2197) scoops out 48 sherbet, sorbet, water ice, and ice cream flavors.

Just beyond the mall's east end is historic **Congress Hall** (251 Beach Ave.), where you'll find antique shops and history-themed souvenir stores. **Beach Avenue,** across the street from the ocean, hosts additional apparel and specialty stores.

RECREATION AND TOURS

Single cruisers and canopied surreys are available at **Shield's Bike Rentals** (11 Guerney St., 609/898-1818, daily 7 A.M.–7 P.M.), located across the street from the city's beachfront Promenade.

Newly relocated at the Nature Center of Cape May, **Aqua Trails** (1600 Delaware Ave., 609/884-5600, www.aquatrails.com) offers guided, sunset, and full-moon kayak nature tours ($46 individual, $80 double), and rents kayaks for use on the bay or the Atlantic. Rental rates are $20 for one hour with an individual kayak and $30 for a double, $75 and $85 for full-day or overnight use. A surf kayak, intended for ocean use, costs $75 for a full day.

Cape May Whale Watcher (609/884-5445 or 800/786-5445, www.capemaywhalewatcher.com) runs two- and three-hour whale and dolphin-watching tours on a 110-foot boat three times daily March–December. Trips leave from the Miss Chris Marina along the Cape May Canal, and cost $28–38 adult, $18–23 child 7–12, age 6 and under free. For wildlife tours along the Cape's backwaters, try **Salt Marsh Safari** (609/884-3100, www.skimmer.com, $27 adult, $15 child). Two-hour trips take place

aboard the Skimmer, a 41-passenger covered pontoon boat. Most depart from Cape May's Dolphin Cove Marina (just beyond the causeway toll bridge heading toward Wildwood Crest) daily at 10 A.M., 1:30 P.M., or 6 P.M. March–December, except Wednesday–Thursday mid-June–Labor Day, when trips depart from Stone Harbor's Wetlands Institute (Thursday's 6 P.M. trip departs from Dolphin Cove).

The Mid-Atlantic Center for the Arts (www.capemaymac.org) runs most Cape May tours. Information and tickets are available at the **Washington Street Mall Information Booth** (429 Washington St., 609/884-2368), staffed with volunteers happy to provide details on the day's offerings. MAC's website also lists updated schedules. Popular MAC tours include day and evening **Trolley Tours, Historic Walking Tours,** and the annual **Christmas Candlelight House Tours,** a regional favorite, so book ahead.

Across the street from the information booth is the boarding stop for the **Cape May Carriage Company** (641 Sunset Blvd., 609/884-4466, www.capemaycarriage.com), offering horse-drawn-carriage historic tours daily in summer (10 A.M.–3 P.M. and 6–10:30 P.M.), and on weekends in spring and fall. Private tours are available in December. Group tour rates are $10 adult, $5 child 2–11. Private carriage rides cost $40 for two passengers, $10 for each additional adult, $5 for an additional child 2–11.

The **Cape May Spa at Congress Hall** (609/898-2429, www.capemaydayspa.com) offers a variety of massages, facials, and bath and body treatments, along with manicures and pedicures. Specialty enhancements include a youthful lip treatment, and aromatherapy.

ENTERTAINMENT AND NIGHTLIFE

Not a nightlife hotspot per se, Cape May hosts several credible options for a good night out.

Locals like to hit up the Marquis De Lafayette's poolside **Fin Bar** (510 Beach Ave., 609/884-3500) late afternoons on their way home from the beach. Then it's on to the nearby **Rusty Nail** (Coachman's Motor Inn, 205 Beach

Ave., 609/884-0220, mid-May–mid-Oct.) for round 2. The Nail is also open daily for breakfast, lunch, and dinner throughout summer. It's quite casual, with live music on weekends. After a quick shower it's on to the evening's third stop, Congress Hall's **Brown Room** (251 Beach Ave., 609/884-8421, open nightly year-round). Not your typical beach establishment, this bar features chocolate-colored walls, a zebra-print rug, a massive stocked bookshelf, and some of the best drinks in town. Its open fireplace is the ideal spot to sit and sip martinis on a winter day. Tucked away in the hotel basement is the trendy **Boiler Room** (609/884-6507, mid-Apr.–Dec.) nightclub. Built into historic Congress Hall's original foundation, this bare-brick-walled and red-lit space is the place to come for dancing, jazz, reggae, and blues.

The **Ugly Mug** (426 Washington St., 609/884-3459, www.uglymugenterprises.com, Mon.–Fri. 10:30 A.M.–midnight, Sat.–Sun. 10:30 A.M.–1 A.M.) is Cape May's best place to chill with a draft any time of the year. Grab a stool at the center bar or slip into a booth, and be sure to bring plenty of change for the jukebox.

Cape May's historic **Beach Theatre** (711 Beach Ave., 800/838-3006) is in trouble. The first-run multiplex—and Cape May's only movie theater—is facing conversion into a mixed-use shopping space, although residents are trying to save it. For ways you can help, visit www.beachtheatre.org.

For a unique experience, try **Elaine's Famous Dinner Theater** (513 Lafayette St., 609/884-4358, www.elainesdinnertheater.com, $39.95 adult, $29.95 teen, $17.95 child), located within Elaine's Victorian Inn. Shows range from silly to scary depending on the season, and all take place throughout a three-course meal. Elaine's also hosts hour-long Victorian Ghost Tours (609/884-4358, $10 adult, $5 child) nightly throughout summer, leaving from the inn.

ACCOMMODATIONS
Hotels

While B&Bs are the crux of Cape May's overnight offerings, there are many hotels and a motel or two that offer the same level of luxury. A stay at one of the following establishments will make your trip just as memorable.

A standout even by Cape May standards is the boutique **Virginia Hotel** (25 Jackson St., 800/732-4236, virginiahotel.com, $290–520), a fully restored 1879 Victorian with 24 stylish guest rooms, each touting Belgian sheets, plasma TVs, terry robes, and minibars. The hotel offers both room service and valet parking, and houses one of the city's finest restaurants downstairs.

For more than 125 years, Cape May's historic 70-room **Chalfonte** (301 Howard St., 609/884-8409 or 888/411-1998, www.chalfonte.com, $217–278) has been welcoming visitors. Guests come to relax on the hotel's wraparound covered porches, dine in its Southern-style restaurant, read in the solarium, and forget about modern worries. You won't find heating, air-conditioning, or amenities like telephones or TVs here, and many of the rooms have shared baths (though they do have in-room sinks). Rates may seem a bit steep for your average getaway, but plenty will find the step back in time worth it. If you're intrigued by the thought but can't part with the cash, the Chalfonte offers spring and fall work weekends ($35 and 10 hours' labor), which include meals and a two-night stay.

Another Cape May beauty, the renovated and restored ◖ **Congress Hall** (251 W. Beach Ave., 609/884-8421 or 888/944-1816, www.congresshall.com, $345–565) once served as a summer White House for President Benjamin Harrison and hosted several other U.S. presidents over the years. In addition to numerous ground-floor shops and a restaurant, a lounge, a nightclub, and a day spa, Congress Hall features 107 modern yet subdued guest rooms that ideally accentuate their historic surrounds. All come with a TV and DVD player, Wi-Fi, and individual climate control, and are within steps to the ocean beach. If crossing the street feels too far, an in-ground pool and adjacent bar are just beyond the back door. Book well ahead for high season.

Bed-and-Breakfasts

Few places rival Cape May when it comes to B&Bs—the city offers one of the best selections on the planet. Many (if not most) of them offer modern guest room amenities such as TV, Wi-Fi, and air-conditioning, although some remain as Victorian as their architecture in terms of up-to-date offerings. Unfortunately, a city law bans the former practice of B&Bs providing complimentary beach tags to guests, although some places will allow visitors to "borrow" their personal stock. Many of the city's overnight establishments require a minimum stay during the high season, and parking is not always provided—it's best to check ahead.

Housed in a restored 1869 Gothic Victorian, **The Abbey** (34 Gurney St., 609/884-4506, www.abbeybedandbreakfast.com, $150–200) features seven period-decorated rooms, each named for an American city. There are plenty of interesting touches, including a displayed hat collection, an S-shaped conversation settee, and pull-chain toilets. Overnight stays come with full breakfast, private bath, and wireless Internet, along with free parking.

Recently expanded to include the former Brass Bed Inn, **The Bacchus Inn** (609/884-2129 or 866/844-2129, www.bacchusinn.com, $155–275) consists of two buildings: the Main House (710 Columbia Ave.), and the Cottage (710 Columbia Ave.). There are 13 rooms between the two, each with its own private bath and wireless Internet, and some with fireplaces and TVs. Named for the Roman god of wine, Bacchus Inn lives up to its moniker by offering complimentary afternoon wine and cheese, but the B&B's biggest perk is its Cottage billiards table.

The 19th-century carpenter Gothic–style **Gingerbread House** (28 Guerney St., 609/884-0211, www.gingerbreadinn.com, $148–298) features six antique-filled guest rooms, some with private baths and all with air-conditioning and flat-screen TVs. Owner and proprietor Fred Echevarria, a self-taught craftsman, has restored each of the inn's bathrooms, adding teakwood and glass shower doors. His handiwork exists throughout the house, along with wife Joan's bright color combos and antique collections.

Spread among two 1880s restored homes and an 1876 gambling parlor, the year-round **🄲 Queen Victoria Bed-and-Breakfast** (102 Ocean St., 609/884-8702, www.queenvictoria.com, $215–305) has everything you might want in a B&B: private baths, wireless Internet, and plentiful porches with rocking chairs and wicker swings. Each of the 32 rooms and suites comes equipped with a flat-screen TV and a fridge, and some have their own entrances. Modern amenities aside, the inn is filled with Victorian touches: period furnishings, handmade quilts, and wallpaper designed by arts and crafts figure William Morris for England's Queen Victoria. Afternoon tea and a breakfast buffet are offered daily.

Built in 1892 by a whaling captain, pretty **Fairthorne Cottage** (111 Ocean St., 609/884-8791 or 800/438-8742, www.fairthorne.com, $230–280) offers eight stylish guest rooms and one suite, all with a TV and VCR and a private bath. This colonial revival inn also features a wonderful wraparound porch lined with rocking chairs, and period decor that doesn't go overboard.

One of Cape May's largest freestanding B&Bs, the **Humphrey Hughes House** (29 Ocean St., 609/884-4428, www.humphreyhugheshouse.com, $299–350) features a sweeping veranda and 10 generously sized Victorian-inspired guest rooms. Amenities include comfy bathrobes and slippers, private baths, air-conditioning, and an on-site library. The elegant **Mainstay Inn** (635 Columbia Ave., 609/884-8690, www.mainstayinn.com, $295–360) consists of two buildings: a cottage and a 19th-century Italian villa once operated as a private gambling club. The two are joined together by a lovely outdoor garden. Guest rooms are filled with Victorian furnishings, some left over from clubhouse days, accented with updated offerings like wireless Internet and flat-screen TVs. In addition to complimentary breakfast, the Mainstay hosts daily afternoon tea, beginning at 4 P.M.

FOOD

Cape May is home to some of New Jersey's best restaurants. The selection is not ethnically diverse, but the quality is impressive. Restaurants run the gamut from beachside breakfast joints to grand Victorian dining rooms, with choices to fit every purse and tax bracket. So eat up; it's worth it.

Casual Eateries

Regardless of their recent franchise offerings, I'm a big fan of the (Ugly Mug (426 Washington St., 609/884-3459, www.uglymug enterprises.com, Mon.–Fri. 10:30 A.M.–midnight, Sat.–Sun. 10:30A.M.–1 A.M. summer, $9–18), a local hangout serving up good American food, cold beer, and camaraderie. There's a well-stocked jukebox in back and a large bar in the center, perfect for whiling away a brisk winter day. Outdoor tables provide endless sightseeing throughout summer months, but if you're headed indoors, request a seat in the original dining room beneath the ceiling of hanging mugs (those of deceased Mug members face seaward)—the authentic atmosphere is worth it. Call ahead for off-season hours.

Cape May's best place for weekend brunch is **The Mad Batter** (19 Jackson St., 609/884-5970, www.madbatter.com, breakfast and lunch daily 8 A.M.–3 P.M., dinner daily from 5 P.M., $19.50–32), situated in the Carroll Villa B&B in downtown's historic district. Request a seat on the front porch for wonderful people-watching while you devour thick slices of orange and almond French toast ($7.50), washed down with fresh-squeezed apple juice ($3).

Tucked into Congress Hall's ground-floor corner is the **Blue Pig Tavern** (Congress Hall, 251 W. Beach Ave., 609/884-8421, breakfast Mon.–Fri. 7:30–11 A.M., Sat.–Sun. 7:30 A.M.–3 P.M., lunch Mon.–Fri. 11 A.M.–2 P.M., Sat.–Sun. 7:30 A.M.–3 P.M., dinner Sun.–Thurs. 5:30–9 P.M., Fri.–Sat. 5:30–10 P.M.), a stylish American eatery serving three meals daily. The restaurant features two distinct dining rooms—one reminiscent of a garden eatery, and the other a cozy tavern spilling onto the outdoor veranda during

summer months. Fish and chips ($15) are a favorite.

Though something of a tourist trap, **The Lobster House** (Fisherman's Wharf, Schellenger Landing, 609/884-8296, call for hours, $18.50–39.95) remains a popular place for family outings, partially due to its dockside location and well-rounded meals. Entrées include shrimp scampi ($20), baked crab imperial ($20), and filet mignon ($25), and include vegetables, potatoes, and salad. There's also an on-site market. Hours vary throughout the year—call ahead.

Locals head to **Louie's Pizza** (711 Beach Ave., 609/884-0305, daily 10 A.M.–10 P.M., $3–17) for pizza pies and slices. Look for it at the start of a side street across from the Promenade.

My sister-in-law grew up in Cape May and swears by **McGlade's** (722 Beach Ave., 609/884-2614, $6–17) as the best breakfast in town. Known for their magnificent omelets, this beachfront property offers an unbeatable view of the Atlantic along with an endless ocean breeze. Open daily throughout the summer.

Fine Dining

Cape May offers some of the state's most rewarding restaurants. Most remain open the majority of the year, though hours tend to cut back gradually after Labor Day. They're really at their peak during July and August, when crowds can be heavy. Reserve your table early.

In business for more than 25 years, **Godmother's Restaurant** (413 S. Broadway, 609/884-4543, www.godmothersrestaurant .com, $16–28) prepares quality Italian dishes, including steak and seafood entrées, incorporating only the freshest Jersey produce. One of the kitchen's best offerings is its mix-and-match pastas and sauces. Godmother's is open daily 5–9 P.M. throughout summer, tapering off to weekends only as the year progresses, and is closed in January.

Serving as the main dining room for Cape May's boutique Virginia Hotel, the award-winning **Ebbitt Room** (25 Jackson St., 609/884-5700, www.virginiahotel.com, nightly

5–9 P.M., $24–34) has been completely renovated and restored to its original Victorian splendor. Highlights include an international wine list and New American dishes that include free range chicken with potato gnocchi ($26) and day-aged sirloin steak for two ($60).

Louisiana-style **410 Bank Street** (410 Bank St., 609/884-2127, daily 5–10 P.M. summer, call for off-season hours, $23–32) is a foodie mainstay and a haven among Manhattanites, serving up French-inspired Creole cuisine in a clapboard-cottage setting. Dining areas include a tropical garden and a vine-covered veranda, although overhead fans cool indoor patrons during summer months. Staff is knowledgeable and there is a small selection of New Jersey wines, otherwise BYO.

Reputed for its outstanding wine selection and a seasonally changing traditional American menu, the **Washington Inn** (801 Washington St., 609/884-5697, www.washingtoninn.com) is Cape May at its best. The restaurant occupies a former 19th-century plantation home in the heart of the city's historic district and features five dining rooms, including a summer patio. Dishes range from a herb crumb–crusted rack of lamb ($34) to pan-seared organic salmon ($27). Washington Inn opens at 5 P.M. daily during summer months, trickling off to weekends only by November; closing hours vary.

Removed from the bustling historic district is the romantic **Peter Shields Restaurant** (1304 W. Beach Ave., 609/884-9090, www.peter shieldsinn.com, nightly from 5 P.M., closed Mon. after Labor Day, $28–36), located on the first floor of the Georgian revival–style Peter Shields Inn. The restaurant features five dining areas, including an ocean-view veranda, and a rotating menu of New American dishes. Drinks are BYO, though a limited selection of Cape May Vineyard wines is available for purchase. A three-course fixed price menu ($38 per person) is offered Sunday–Thursday before 6 P.M.

GETTING THERE AND AROUND

Both Cape May and nearby Cape May Point are situated at the Garden State Parkway's southernmost point. To reach downtown Cape May from Wildwood Crest, take Route 621 (Ocean Drive) south over the causeway bridge and turn east onto Route 109 (Lafayette Street). Cape May Point is reachable from downtown Cape May by taking Sunset Boulevard west.

To reach either locale from South Jersey, take Route 47 (from Philly, take Route 42 to Route 55, which runs into Route 47) to Route 9 South and follow the signs to Cape May.

CAPE MAY POINT

Only 10 minutes west of Cape May City, the less-than-one-square-mile borough of Cape May Point has a decidedly different feel. With one general store and no bed-and-breakfasts, not to mention strict zoning laws keeping most homes for single-family use, the Point is quieter, less touristy, and more in tune with its natural surrounds. There are good opportunities for kayaking and sailing in local waters, and the Point offers one of the most varied and prolific birding opportunities in the entire country. Keep an eye out for hawks, falcons, eagles, ducks, geese, and herons, to name a few. In addition, Cape May Point is home to a state park, a lighthouse, one of New Jersey's most serene beaches, and tiny chunks of collectible quartz crystals found nowhere else on earth.

Cape May Point State Park

Windswept dunes, coastal woodlands, and freshwater marshes and ponds make up 235-acre Cape May Point State Park (Lighthouse Ave., Cape May Point, 609/884-2159, free), a key attraction on New Jersey's Coastal Heritage Trail. Constructed boardwalks and viewing platforms are great places for spotting waterfowl, songbirds, shorebirds, and raptors migrating through the area annually. The park is home to the romantic **Cape May Lighthouse,** a whitewashed tower standing 157 feet tall and that's more than 150 years old. One hundred ninety-nine cast-iron steps lead to a 360-degree lookout balcony, just below the active beacon. Both the lighthouse and the beach beneath are popular spots for couples to get engaged. The lighthouse is open for self-guided tours ($5 adult, $1 child) daily April–November, and usually on weekends the rest of the year. Just off the shore stands an old World War II defense bunker being battered by the sea.

In 2004–2005 the Army Corps of Engineers pumped the beach with millions of yards of sand to save migrating wildlife, concurrently rescuing it for public use from long Jersey Shore erosion.

Sunset Beach

The only beach in New Jersey where the sun both rises and sets over the Atlantic Ocean, Sunset Beach (800/757-6468, www.sunset beachnj.com) is also the only beach in the state (and the world) where you can find Cape May diamonds, bits of quartz crystals churned into creation by the sea. These tiny rocklike gems (you have to get 'em polished to make 'em sparkle) are sprinkled throughout the sand, plentiful and free. It is a gorgeous little beach, home to a cluster of shops and a flag-lowering ceremony held every evening at dusk. Fifty yards into the water are the still-visible remains of the *Atlantus,* a World War I concrete ship that the sea continues to slowly swallow.

Shop for candles, collectibles, and calendars, along with local literature and Shore-related tunes at **Sunset Beach Gift Shop** (502 Sunset Blvd., 609/884-7079). While Cape May jewelers will polish your diamond finds, you can purchase them here pre-polished for only a couple of dollars. The shop also sells necklaces, earrings, and rings adorned with Cape May diamonds. Additional Sunset Beach retailers include an apparel store and fossil shop, as well as a grill.

Higbee Beach

Just around the bend west of Sunset Beach is 1.5-mile Higbee Beach, a crescent-shaped sliver of white sand scattered with driftwood and lined by smooth blue ocean. In early summer dozens of horseshoe crab armors, their occupants victims of hungry shorebirds, often overtake the shore. Except for the ferry leaving for Delaware's Rehoboth Beach from the visible Cape May Canal, this beach feels truly remote,

perhaps the reason it operated as a nude beach (it no longer is) for so many years. Quiet and peaceful, it's an ideal getaway from the bustle happening along much of the Jersey Shore.

A coastal forest of holly, cedars, beach plums, and brush fields separates the parking area from the beach. In addition to straightaway access there are several nature trails within. Both the beach and the forest are part of the **Higbee Beach Wildlife Management Area** (609/628-2103, daily 5 A.M.–9 P.M.). Higbee Beach is dog-friendly.

Cape May–Lewes Ferry

One of the best routes into Cape May is aboard a ferry. The car and passenger Cape May–Lewes Ferry (Sandman Blvd. and Lincoln Dr., North Cape May, 800/643-3779, www.cape-maylewesferry.com) links the Cape May region to Delaware's Lewes, seven miles north of the Rehoboth Beach resort. Ferries run round-trip year-round (schedules vary seasonally) and take about 70 minutes each way. One-way fares are $7–9.50 adult, $3.50–4.75 child for vehicle and foot passengers, $28–34 for a car and driver, with discounts offered for round-trip fares. Shuttles to and from the ferry cost $3 for those age 6 and older.

Cape May Bird Observatory

Greater Cape May is a birder's paradise; the Audubon Center alone runs two local outposts, each part of the larger Cape May Bird Observatory. The first is **Northwood Center** (701 East Lake Dr., 609/884-2736, Thurs.–Mon. 9 A.M.–4:30 P.M.), located just up the road from the Cape May Lighthouse, and the second is Route 47's **Center for Research and Education** (609/861-0700, daily 1–4:30 P.M.), a model exhibit for creating your backyard wilderness, replete with hummingbirds. The observatory hosts public programs such as nature walks, butterfly and birding tours, and popular Back Bay Birding by Boat excursions at various times throughout the year. For details on where to meet and how to register, visit the Audubon Observatory website at www.njaudubon.org/Centers/CMBO, or call the Cape May Natural

History and Events Hotline at 609/861-0466. For updates on recent regional bird sightings dial 609/898-2473.

The **Nature Center of Cape May** (1600 Delaware Ave., 609/898-8848, www.nj audubon.org/Centers/NCCM, Tues.–Sat. 10 A.M.–3 P.M. Sept.–May, daily 9 A.M.–4 P.M. June–Aug.) is the Audubon Society's official local home, hosting several educational and volunteer programs year-round.

World Series of Birding

Never heard of the World Series of Birding (609/884-2736, www.njaudubon.org/WSB)? You're missing out. This annual Audubon event sees hundreds of teams competing to spot the most birds over a 24-hour period in May. Birding can be done one of two ways: either on a regulated platform, or by travel within a specified region. Everyone in the group has to see the bird for it to count, and teams must check in with their lists at Cape May Point State Park before the 24 hours are up. Think you can identify a Louisiana water thrush or a yellow-throated warbler? Then sign up: The competition's open to everyone.

Camping

Close to Cold Spring Village and minutes from downtown Cape May, 175-acre **Cape Island Resort** (709 Rte. 9, Cape May, 609/884-5777 or 800/437-7443, www.capeisland.com, May–Nov., from $30) hosts two large swimming pools, recreation facilities, and sites for both tents and RVs.

A bit north is **Seashore Campsites** (720 Seashore Rd., Cape May, 609/884-4010, www .seashorecampsites.com, mid-Apr.–Oct.), a 600-site resort tucked onto 90 wooded acres, complete with billiard tables, a heated pool, and a lake with its own bathing beach. Religious services are held on-site seasonally. Sites begin at $28 May–mid-June, $52 mid-June–August.

ROUTE 9: SOMERS POINT–CAPE MAY COURT HOUSE

More scenic than the Garden State Parkway and faster than Ocean Drive, Route 9 offers

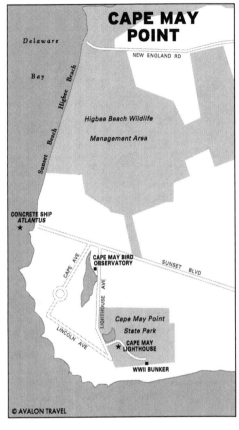

its own array of attractions, including numerous seasonal ice cream stands and miniature golf courses. The stretch is also home to several hotels and camping resorts offering affordable alternatives to Shore towns. Though the roadway really comes alive during summer months (including often-heavy traffic), many of the antique stores leading to the lower route's "Antique Alley" remain open throughout winter. Beyond the Cape, Route 9 continues north into Atlantic County, passing Smithville and Brigantine Wildlife Refuge onto Forked River and Tuckerton, en route to Toms River.

Cold Spring Village

Cold Spring (720 Rte. 9, 609/898-2300, www

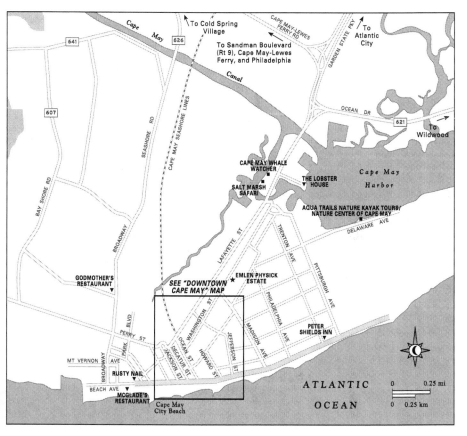

.hcsv.org, Sat.–Sun. 10:30 A.M.–4:30 P.M. Memorial Day–mid-June and Labor Day–mid-Sept., and Tues.–Sun. 10:30 A.M.–4:30 P.M. mid-June–Labor Day, $8 adult, $5 child) is the Cape's living history museum, a re-created 19th-century outdoor museum with 25 restored buildings and costumed interpreters demonstrating traditional crafts like bookbinding, weaving, and basket-making. The village houses both an ice cream parlor and an American restaurant (Wed.–Sun.), along with farm animals and a depot for the **Seashore Lines Train** (www.seashorelines.com, 609/884-2675, $5 adult, $4 child round-trip), which runs a loop between downtown Cape May and Cape May Zoo during high season.

Photographers may want to pit-stop at the striking **Cold Spring Cemetery** (780 Seashore Rd.), a Presbyterian cemetery open to all denominations located nearby.

Cape May National Wildlife Refuge

To see migratory flycatchers, orioles, tanagers, and endangered piping plovers in their natural habitat, visit Cape May National Wildlife Refuge (24 Kimbles Beach Rd., Cape May Court House, 609/463-0994, www.fws.gov/northeast/capemay). Opened in 1989, the refuge is home or temporary lodging for hundreds of bird species and dozens of reptiles, mammals, and amphibians, along with strictly sea creatures. During fall the refuge welcomes upwards of 15 raptor species. A handful of nature trails ideal for wildlife spotting and nature photography spread throughout the property. The headquarters are open Monday–Friday 8 A.M.–4:30 P.M., and the trails are open to the public daily.

Cape May County Zoo

Both kids and parents are fans of the free Cape May County Zoo (Rte. 9 and Pine Ln., 609/465-5271, www.capemaytimes.com/cape-may-county/zoo, daily 10 A.M.–4:45 P.M. summer, call for off-season hours), home to more than 100 animal species, including red pandas, giraffes, camels, bison, and tigers. Though small children may find the reptile house a bit scary, they'll flip over the new enclosed World of Birds. The zoo's part of a larger 200-acre wooded park filled with walking paths, fishing ponds, and playgrounds.

Cape May Court House

Don't let the name fool you. Cape May Court House is actually a town located along Route 9 north of Cape May Point. Downtown hosts a charming stretch of antique stores and small cafés. It's a good place for grabbing a cup of coffee. If you have time, stop by the **Cape May County Historical Museum** (504 Rte. 9 N., 609/465-3535, www.cmcmuseum.org) to learn about local maritime history and the Lenni-Lenape Indians.

Leaming's Run Gardens

With 25 themed gardens, an arboretum, a bamboo grove, bridges, ponds, and more, Leaming's Run (1845 Rte. 9 N., Swainton, 609/465-5871, www.leamingsrungardens.com, daily 9:30 A.M.–5 P.M. mid-May–mid-Oct., $8 adult, $4 child) comprises the country's largest annual gardens. Visitors can stroll among 30 acres and along a mile-long meandering walking path to view ever-changing flower displays, rediscover the 18th-century Colonial Farm, spot native frogs and turtles, and relax amid August's buzz of migrating ruby-throated hummingbirds. In late October Leaming's Run morphs into Screamings Run, hosting haunted candlelit tours (609/465-5871, $7) along the pathway.

Information and Services

A good site for gathering details on local happenings is **www.capemay.com.** Information is also available at **The Chamber of Commerce of Greater Cape May** (www.capemaychamber .com), which hosts the **Cape May Welcome & Information Center** (609 Lafayette St., 609/884-9562) in the city's downtown. **Cape May County Department of Tourism** (609/463-6415 or 800/227-2297) is accessible on the Web at www.thejerseycape.net.

MOON THE JERSEY SHORE
Avalon Travel
a member of the Perseus Books Group
1700 Fourth Street
Berkeley, CA 94710, USA
www.moon.com

Editor: Elizabeth Hollis Hansen
Series Manager: Kathryn Ettinger
Copy Editor: Christopher Church
Graphics Coordinators: Kathryn Osgood,
   Stefano Boni
Production Coordinator: Darren Alessi
Cover Designer: Kathryn Osgood
Map Editor: Kevin Anglin
Cartographers: Kat Bennett, Chris Markiewicz
Cartography Director: Mike Morgenfeld

ISBN-13: 978-1-59880-273-3

Text © 2009 by Laura Kiniry.
Maps © 2009 by Avalon Travel.
All rights reserved.

Some photos and illustrations are used by permission and are the property of the original copyright owners.

Front cover photo: Pink bicycles on boardwalk © Andrew Kazmierski/dreamstime.com
Title page photo: Lucy The Elephant © Save Lucy Commitee, Inc. 2005 All rights reserved.

Printed in the United States

Moon Handbooks and the Moon logo are the property of Avalon Travel. All other marks and logos depicted are the property of the original owners. All rights reserved. No part of this book may be translated or reproduced in any form, except brief extracts by a reviewer for the purpose of a review, without written permission of the copyright owner.

Although every effort was made to ensure that the information was correct at the time of going to press, the author and publisher do not assume and hereby disclaim any liability to any party for any loss or damage caused by errors, omissions, or any potential travel disruption due to labor or financial difficulty, whether such errors or omissions result from negligence, accident, or any other cause.

ABOUT THE AUTHOR

Laura Kiniry

© MATTHEW JONES

Laura Kiniry knows New Jersey like only a native could – spending post-prom at Atlantic City casinos, weekending in Wildwood, attending the Miss America Pageant, walking the boards of Ocean City, and devouring diner cheese fries at 2 A.M. Her one regret is never making it inside the now-extinct Brigantine Castle. For Laura, the perfect evening is a salty summer night down the shore, with a ride on the Wonderland carousel and a tub of Johnson's popcorn.

Laura's work has appeared in a variety of publications, including *National Geographic Traveler, Bicycling, AARP, Craft,* and *Backstreets,* the Springsteen fanzine. She took her first international trip to Scandinavia at age 16 and has since continued to explore – bungee jumping in New Zealand, trekking in Thailand, braving the Australian Outback, working a summer at Glacier National Park, and traversing the United States by train numerous times.

Laura currently resides in San Francisco, California, but she remains a Jersey girl through and through.